BOTTICELLI

BOTTICELLI

SUSAN LEGOUIX

BLOOMSBURY BOOKS
LONDON

(frontispiece)
Venus and Mars (detail of Plate 61)

ACKNOWLEDGEMENTS

I am especially grateful to Allan Braham of the National Gallery for making the Eastlake notebooks available to me and for his useful comments on the Merton portrait; Peter Dreyer of the Staatliche Museen, West Berlin; Christa Gardner; Martin Kemp of Glasgow University for generously allowing me to read his article on the Glasgow *Annunciation* prior to publication; Lady Merton for permission to reproduce the *Portrait of a Young Man Holding a Medallion*; Joyce Plesters of the National Gallery for information on Botticelli's technique and Christopher Wright for encouraging me to undertake the whole project.

Sincere thanks are also due to the following for their help in providing photographs and information: Accademia Carrara, Bergamo; Alte Pinakothek, Munich; Biblioteca Apostolica Vaticana, Vatican City; Bildarchiv Preussischer Kulturbesitz, Berlin; British Museum, London; Capilla Real, Granada; City Art Gallery, Birmingham; Church of Sant' Anna dei Lombardi, Naples; Church of Santa Maria Novella, Florence; Fratelli Alinari, Florence; Gabinetto Fotografico Nazionale, Rome; Galleria degli Uffizi, Florence; Gallerie Nazionale di Capodimonte, Naples; Galleria Pallavicini-Rospigliosi, Rome; Isabella Stewart Gardner Museum, Boston; Glasgow Art Gallery, Glasgow; Metropolitan Museum of Art, New York; Monastery of Ognissanti, Florence; Musée du Louvre, Paris; Museo del' Opera del Duomo, Florence; Museo del Prado, Madrid; Museo Poldi-Pezzoli, Milan; National Gallery, London; National Gallery of Art, Washington; National Gallery of Scotland, Edinburgh; Oronoz S.A., Madrid; Philadelphia Museum of Art, Philadelphia; Pinacoteca Ambrosiana, Milan; Service de Documentation Photographique de la Réunion des Musées Nationaux, Paris; Staatliche Gemäldegalerie, Berlin; Staatliche Gemäldegalerie, Dresden.

For Ron

This edition published 1987 by
Bloomsbury Books an imprint of
Godfrey Cave Associates Limited
42 Bloomsbury Street, London WC1B 3QJ
under license from Minotaur Publishing Co Ltd

ISBN 1 870630 25 4

Printed in Yugoslavia

Sandro Botticelli

THIS BOOK ILLUSTRATES over sixty paintings by Botticelli. Only one, *The Mystic Nativity* (Plate IV), is signed and dated, and only one group, the Sistine Chapel frescoes (Plates V and 30–36), is still in its original position. We know almost nothing about the life and character of the artist, and there is an awkward period of almost ten years at the end of his life when, for reasons as yet unknown, he seems to have abandoned painting altogether.

Such an accumulation of negative factors might be a deterrent to further investigation were it not for the magic of the images which survive. Botticelli's art has proved more magnetic to historians and critics during the past hundred years than that of any other fifteenth-century painter. Over forty serious studies have found a place on library shelves, and almost half as many picture books occupy the coffee tables and bookcases of the art lovers of the world.

The very high survival rate of Botticelli's work compensates for the lack of documentation. Sixty or so paintings, a collection of drawings and many associated studio works is a surprisingly large *oeuvre* for such an early master, and it enables us to make an assessment of his style which is likely to be far better balanced than our view of the work of a painter such as the ill-fated Mantegna who is represented today by only a tiny proportion of his original output.

The city of Florence and the quality of life it offered in the fifteenth century made Botticelli's work what it is. Florence was his birthplace and the town where he spent the whole of his life apart from a short visit to Pisa in 1474 and about a year spent in Rome from 1481–82. The Ognissanti region of Florence, where his family the Filipepi were tanners, was the centre of the wool-working industry. The Vespucci, near neighbours of the Filipepi and patrons of Botticelli, were most important in their own time as dealers in wool and silk, but are best remembered for the fact that Amerigo, one of their sons, gave a name to the New World. Their house and the one that Botticelli occupied for most of his life were in the Via del Porcellana which runs between Borgo Ognissanti and Via Palazzuolo (see map, pages 18–19). Vasari recounted a story which if it can be relied upon gives us a rare glimpse of Botticelli's character, and even if it is not altogether true does illustrate vividly the hazards of living amidst the busy fabric in-

dustry. A cloth weaver moved eight looms into the house next door to Botticelli's and so disturbed the artist with the deafening sound and vibration of his machines that work became impossible. Gaining no favourable response from his polite request for a little peace and quiet, Botticelli was finally driven to take desperate retaliatory action. On a high wall at the side of his house he balanced an enormous stone in such a position that at any suggestion of vibration it threatened to crash through the weaver's roof. The result was, according to Vasari, that the neighbour was forced to mend his ways and come to an amicable agreement with Botticelli.

Artists' workshops were themselves 'home industries' and by 1472 when Botticelli's name first appeared in the record books of the painters' guild he already had an assistant, the fifteen- or sixteen-year-old Filippino Lippi, son of Filippo Lippi who had died a few years earlier in 1469. By 1480 Botticelli's studio was firmly established and in a legal declaration of that year he listed three assistants, Raffaello di Lorenzo di Frosino Tosi, Giovanni di Benedetto Gianfanini and Jacopo di Domenico Papi. Elsewhere assistants named Jacopo, Biagio and Ludovico are mentioned, but the only one to emerge as an artist of individual talent was Filippino Lippi. Botticelli's own training in the 1460s appears to have taken place in the studio of Filippino's father Filippo Lippi. Certain features of his earliest pictures such as the architectural setting of the *Madonna and Child in an Archway* (Plate 2) and the *Madonna and Child with Two Angels* (Plate 3) can be seen to have been directly derived from models by Lippi, and Botticelli's sweet-faced women, so effusively praised in the literature of the early part of the twentieth century, are the natural descendants of Lippi's Madonnas and female saints.

In addition to Lippi the artists who made the most impression on the young painter were the Pollaiuolo brothers (fig. 1), with whom he worked in the hall of the Arte della Mercanzia (see Plate 6), and Verrocchio, the master of Leonardo. The influence of Verrocchio is most apparent in the early Madonna and Child pictures, such as those in the Uffizi (Plates 1 and 2), Naples (Plate 3) and Boston (Plate 4). These Madonnas wear robes and headdresses very similar to those of Verrocchio's Madonnas in the *Madonna and Child* in the

fig. 1 Antonio and Piero POLLAIUOLO
Charity
Florence, Galleria degli Uffizi. Tempera on panel.

The Pollaiuolo brothers were responsible for paintings of the six Virtues, Faith, Hope, Charity, Temperence, Prudence and Justice, and Botticelli for the seventh, Fortitude, for the hall of the Arte della Mercanzia in Florence. It is generally believed that Piero Pollaiuolo painted *Charity* and the other panels, but scholars also believe that his brother Antonio had a hand in the designs of the figures. A comparison between this picture and Botticelli's *Fortitude* (Plate 6) shows how Botticelli imitated certain elements of the Pollaiuolo stylistic language, in particular the mannered treatment of hands and feet. Botticelli's figure, however, sits much more naturally on her throne than the *Charity* or any of the other *Virtues*.

Staatliche Gemäldegalerie, Berlin (Dahlem) (fig. 2), and *The Ruskin Madonna*, now in the National Gallery of Scotland, Edinburgh (fig. 3). The facial features of the Madonnas in these pictures by Verrocchio and Botticelli are also strikingly alike. The relationship with Antonio and Piero Pollaiuolo is discernible mainly in the drawing of male figures and in the articulation of the limbs of figures in movement (fig. 4). The sinuous form of Holofernes in *The Finding of the Dead Holofernes* (Plate 54), which was probably painted around 1470, the period of the decorations in the hall of the Arte della Mercanzia, is reminiscent of nudes by Antonio Pollaiuolo, but by the time Botticelli painted the reclining Mars in *Venus and Mars* (Plate 61) in the late 1480s, the influence was no longer important. Similarities with Verrocchio also cease to be noticeable in the pictures of the 1480s although the pretty, feminine spirit of Lippi lingered and played a part in Botticelli's style until his latest period of the 1490s.

Filippo Lippi was lucky enough to be one of the generation of artists befriended and patronized by

fig. 2 Andrea del VERROCCHIO
Madonna and Child
Berlin (Dahlem), Staatliche Gemäldegalerie. Tempera on panel.

The Madonna in this picture and *The Ruskin Madonna* (fig. 3) are clearly related to early pictures by Botticelli such as the *Madonna and Child in an Archway* (Plate 2) and the *Madonna and Child with Symbols of the Eucharist* (Plate 4).

Cosimo 'il Vecchio' de' Medici, and Botticelli had equal good fortune in that his coming of age as a painter coincided with the assumption of Cosimo's grandson, Lorenzo 'il Magnifico', to the leadership of the Medici family and its party on the death of his father, Piero 'the Gouty', in 1469. It is not known precisely how much work Botticelli executed for the Palazzo Medici in Florence, but an inventory made at the time of Lorenzo's death in 1492 records a *Fortuna* and a standard decorated with a *Pallas* made for a famous tournament organized by the Medici in the Piazza Santa Croce in 1475. In addition, Vasari mentioned portraits of Lucrezia Tornabuoni, mother of Lorenzo de' Medici, and of Simonetta Vespucci and a *Bacchus*, all hanging in various parts of the Palazzo Medici. Like the decorative frescoes painted for the Medici family at their country villas of Spedaletto, near Volterra, and Castello, just outside Florence, these works are all lost. Happily three major paintings commissioned by Lorenzo's second cousin Lorenzo di Pierfrancesco de' Medici do survive, *Pallas and the Centaur* (Plate 63), *Primavera* (Plate 65) and *The Birth of Venus* (Plate 66). All three are believed to have been executed for the Villa di Castello. They were only removed from there and seen for the first time by the public in the nineteenth century. Botticelli's relationship with Lorenzo di Pierfrancesco appears to have been very close. In 1496 when the Medici administration was on the point of collapse and any written communication to the family was in danger of being intercepted by political opponents, Michelangelo despatched a letter to Lorenzo di Pierfrancesco addressed to 'Sandro di bottjcello in firenze'. The trust between this member of the Medici

family and Botticelli was of particular importance as it gave the artist the freedom he required to produce his most original and extraordinary work, the illustrated *Divina Commedia* (Plates 70–73).

Although the two pictures most familiar today, *Primavera* and *The Birth of Venus*, were Medici commissions, most of Botticelli's time and energy was devoted to working for the Church, as can be seen from a glance at the map of Florence on pages 18–19 illustrating the original distribution of the pictures in the city. As Botticelli undertook no multiple-panel altar pieces there are practically no reconstructions of altar pieces or fresco cycles to be made and historians have tended

fig. 3 Andrea del VERROCCHIO
Madonna and Child (*The Ruskin Madonna*)
Edinburgh, National Gallery of Scotland.
Tempera transferred from panel to canvas.

Although this picture is very closely related to other Madonna and Child groups attributed to Verrocchio, it has also been proposed that it might be an early work of Leonardo da Vinci executed in Verrocchio's workshop.

fig. 4 Antonio POLLAIUOLO
Battle of Nude Men
London, Victoria and Albert Museum
(Department of Prints and Drawings).
Engraving.

Although Botticelli's early development reflected the influence of Pollaiuolo the nudes in this 'battle' illustrate an obsessive interest in dynamic movement which is very different from the grace of, for instance, Botticelli's *St. Sebastian* (Plate 7).

to pay little attention to the sites in Florence for which many of the pictures were painted, though on occasions they may have a bearing on the final appearance of the work. The Berlin *St. Sebastian* (Plate 7) is an interesting case. It hung originally, we are told, 'in una colonna' in the Church of Santa Maria Maggiore, and the deduction that the picture is tall and narrow because it hung on a pillar, though fundamental, is only one of the conclusions which follows. Santa Maria Maggiore is a three-aisled hall, one of the oldest churches in Florence, supported by solid quadrangular piers which measure 87·5 cm. in width at eye level. The first column on the right is frescoed with two tiers of full-length saints, probably executed by two or more different fourteenth-century artists. The lower tier of the east face of this pier is occupied by an *Execution of St. Sebastian*. Since representations of archers as well as of the saint himself had to be fitted into the limited space, the individual figure of St. Sebastian is half the size of the other seven saints decorating this column. The composition is crowded and uncomfortably out of scale with the other figures, and it is quite feasible that Botticelli's own recognition of the shortcomings of this earlier painting led him to make his *St. Sebastian* for the same church a single figure composition. It is even possible that Botticelli's panel was made to hang over the fresco, but as yet no record has been found of who commissioned his painting.

The Bardi Altarpiece (Plate 9) of 1485, now in Berlin, is another picture which may have been influenced by the nature of its original location. It occupied the first altar on the left on the back wall of the chancel in Santo Spirito. There is not a great deal of evidence that Botticelli was an artist particularly sensitive to the fall of light, but the direction of the light source in the Bardi Chapel does coincide with that in the picture. What may be more significant is the architecture, or lack of architecture, in the composition. Brunelleschi's Santo Spirito was one of the great new churches of Florence, a model for architects of Botticelli's generation. Rather than compete with Brunelleschi and place his figures in their own architectural setting, as did, for example, Cosimo Roselli in his *Madonna Enthroned* of 1482 nearby in the transept, Botticelli constructed rich leafy arches which serve the function of architecture in framing and setting off the figures, but which bear no relation to any building style. There is every indication that the picture is one of the most painstakingly composed and executed of the artist's works and so it is not altogether surprising to learn that the frame, now lost, was made by Giuliano da Sangallo, the eminent architect who only a few years later was working on the fabric of Santo Spirito, building the sacristy. A tondo still furnished with an original frame, *The Virgin and Child with St. John and an Angel* (fig. 5) in London, is inscribed on the back [M?] *Giuljano da san Ghallo*, which may signify another case of collaboration between the two artists.

For making the frame of *The Bardi Altarpiece* Sangallo received almost a third as much as Botticelli was paid for painting the picture. But these figures are misleading unless examined in more detail. Of Botticelli's seventy-eight florins, thirty-eight were for the gold and gilding of the altarpiece, and of Sangallo's twenty-four florins a fair proportion must have been spent on materials. What emerges from the figures is the high price paid for embellishments. Of a total of 102 florins paid by Agnolo Bardi for the altarpiece only thirty-five florins went towards the artist's brushwork. The picture would not of course have been the same without the embellishments. The decorative character of Botticelli's art has always been recognized as one of its greatest qualities, though in the present century a preoccupation with iconographical questions has tended to override considerations of the glory of ornamentation. The astute Herbert Horne, whose monograph on Botticelli is an essential point of departure for all later studies, observed that in nineteenth-century England 'The pictures of Botticelli and his school, like those of Crivelli, were sought out for their decorative beauty before their finer and more artistic traits had been duly appreciated, or even realised.'

Horne's coupling of the names of Botticelli and Crivelli is not merely fortuitous. Subconsciously he pinpointed a deeper truth about the place of Botticelli in history. In an age when we are conditioned to search for historical and artistic developments, it is disturbingly difficult to accommodate neatly the work of Crivelli and Botticelli. Both occupy their own private culs-de-sac. By the end of Crivelli's life Titian was almost ten years old and by Botticelli's death in 1510 Raphael was working on the Stanze of the Vatican and Michelangelo on the ceiling of the Sistine Chapel. If few pictures survived by Crivelli or Botticelli we could be forgiven for imagining that Crivelli might have worked towards a style which looked finally something like that of the early Titian, and that Botticelli's late work looked rather Raphaelesque. Yet the reality is that if any of Botticelli's work looks remotely Raphaelesque it is that of his middle rather than of his late period, and that the passage of time sees his art and that of Crivelli move into a distinctly Gothic idiom.

If it is true of any artist it is true of Botticelli that his art was a personal statement. It can be enjoyed for its own sake regardless of its place in any pattern of development which historians with hindsight project as to the period and style to which it belongs. Yet doggedly we pursue the quest for a wider significance, with varying degrees of success depending on our interpretive skills. Wölfflin, whose particular objective was 'classic' art, wrote: 'He [Botticelli] succeeds in imparting this flowing line to his large masses, and where he orders his picture in a unified composition around one centre something specifically new is created, the consequences of which are of great importance. It is in this sense that his compositions of *The Adoration of the Magi* are to be considered.' It may not be especially helpful to seek out these 'consequences', but an examination and comparison of the five surviving Adoration and Nativity pictures does reveal many of the nuances of Botticelli's personal style over the thirty-year period of his working life. Visitors to London are fortunate enough to be able to see three of these five pictures hanging in the same room in the National Gallery. The remaining two are in the Uffizi, Florence, and the National Gallery of Art, Washington.

The earliest of the Adorations is the small but wide panel in London (Plate 17). The Virgin and Child are placed to one side of the picture and a huge crowd of figures led by the Magi stream away from them. The scheme is much the same as that used by Gentile da Fabriano as early as 1423 in his famous *Adoration of the Magi* now in the Uffizi (fig. 6). Like Gentile, Botticelli made his first king kneel to kiss the toe of Christ and the second kneel and remove his crown. The figure style adopted by Botticelli in the picture is very close to that

fig. 5 Studio of BOTTICELLI
The Virgin and Child with St. John and an Angel
London, National Gallery. Tempera on panel.
Original frame.

Although this is generally acknowledged today to be a studio piece it is a most appealing picture, competently executed. Similar shiny haloes appear in a *Madonna and Child Embraced by St. John* in the Pitti Palace, Florence, which may be by the same hand.

fig. 6 Gentile da FABRIANO
The Adoration of the Magi
Florence, Galleria degli Uffizi. Tempera on panel.

This glorious altarpiece would have been seen by Botticelli in the Strozzi Chapel in Santa Trinità, Florence, where it originally hung.

fig. 7 Studio of BOTTICELLI
The Holy Family
Boston, Isabella Stewart Gardner Museum. Tempera on panel.

This picture is composed of a curious patchwork of styles, and it has even been suggested that the massive St. Joseph is the work of the young Michelangelo.

of Lippi, so close that many scholars agree with Horne that this is 'one very early painting' by the artist, probably done soon after he left his master's studio. The highly experimental nature of the technique, apparent in the numerous revisions of certain areas of *The Adoration*, and the struggle which has gone into the depiction of the architecture are additional signs of immaturity, but the picture could not be called incompetent. The characterization of the figures is remarkably varied and expressive. Two young shepherds who make a speedy entry on the right are related to a pair who appear with rather less verve in a much later studio picture in the Isabella Stewart Gardner Museum, Boston (fig. 7). Their origin is mysterious. Mantegna introduced a similar but more uncouth pair on the right-hand side of his *Adoration of the Shepherds* of about 1450 in the Metropolitan Museum, New York

fig. 8 Andrea MANTEGNA
The Adoration of the Shepherds
New York, Metropolitan Museum of Art.
Tempera transferred from panel to canvas.

fig. 9 Antonio ROSELLINO
The Nativity
Naples, Church of Sant' Anna dei Lombardi.
Marble relief.

Antonio Rosellino carved this relief in the
1470s as the altarpiece for the tomb chapel of
Maria of Aragón in the Church of Sant' Anna
dei Lombardi. The work was carried out in
Florence and then transported to Naples. It
has been suggested that the shepherds could
have been influenced by Hugo van der Goes's
Portinari Altarpiece, but it is now known that
this did not arrive in Florence until 1483,
after Rosellino's death.

(fig. 8), as did Antonio Rosellino in his relief *Nativity* in
Naples (fig. 9) of the 1470s.

The tondo *Adoration of the Magi* in London (Plate III)
repeats a number of the figures from the first picture,
such as the man to the extreme left who blows his nose,
but it is certainly a work of greater maturity. The
success of the composition can only be fully realized if
it is placed against an earlier circular Adoration such
as that by Filippo Lippi in the National Gallery of Art,
Washington (fig. 10). Whereas Lippi simply condensed
the traditional rectangular grouping, Botticelli moved

fig. 10 Filippo LIPPI
The Adoration of the Magi
Washington, National Gallery of Art (Samuel
H. Kress collection). Tempera on panel.

This picture of about 1445 is an early, if not
the earliest, tondo Adoration composition. It is
thought to have been conceived and perhaps
partially executed by Fra Angelico and completed by Filippo Lippi. It is not known where
in Florence it originally hung.

the Virgin right back into the centre of the circle and
allowed her to be smaller than the foreground members
of the crowd. Attention is skilfully focused on her by the
grouping of the surrounding figures and by the arrangement of the monumental ruined architecture which
soars above.

The figures in the third *Adoration of the Magi* (Plate
21) in the Uffizi are much larger in scale than those in
the two London pictures, but even so they must have
been dwarfed by the vast interior of Santa Maria
Novella where the picture originally was. Vasari called
it 'a truly admirable work, executed so beautifully, in
colouring, drawing, and composition, that every crafts-
man today marvels at it'. He pointed out that most of
the figures in the picture are portraits of the Medici
family and their entourage. It must have been the call
for portraits in the commission, in addition to the size
of the church, which dictated the scale of the figures.
In order to represent each person as clearly as possible
Botticelli not only made each larger than his counterpart in the London pictures, but he also placed the

fig. 11 DONATELLO
St. John the Evangelist
Florence, Museo del' Opera del Duomo.
Marble.

A drawing by a Florentine artist of the second
half of the sixteenth century in the Museo
del' Opera del Duomo shows sculptures of the
four Evangelists flanking the great west door
of Florence Cathedral. Donatello's *St. John*
was on the right-hand side nearest the door.

group on a slight slope so that the heads could be seen
above each other. This picture was painted around
1475–77, perhaps only five or six years after the
London tondo. The increase of naturalism in Botticelli's
style during this period can be demonstrated by a comparison of the horse's head on the left of the composition

(Plate 22) with horses in the London pictures. Instead
of being a formalized creature apparently drawn from
Antique sculpture, the horse in the Uffizi *Adoration* is a
tactile quivering beast who nuzzles at the arm of his
owner. The Madonna presenting her child to the oldest
king, a portrait of Cosimo de' Medici, differs very little
from the earlier representations of her. Her curiously
extended torso suggests that Botticelli might have used
sculptural models such as Donatello's *St. John* (fig. 11)
for studies of seated figures. It is usually supposed that
the *St. John* was deliberately made very tall so that in
his original position on the façade of the Duomo the
figure appeared in proportion when seen from the
ground. But Donatello surely over-compensated, for
the *St. John* sat in the lowest row of niches, and if an
artist were to place himself at a comfortable distance to
draw the sculpture he would have seen a figure with an
exaggeratedly tall body and short legs, rather like
Botticelli's seated Madonnas.

Vasari said of the Uffizi *Adoration* that it brought
Botticelli considerable fame, both in Florence and
further afield and led to the call to Rome to work in
the Sistine Chapel. The fourth of the known Adoration
pictures, the one now in Washington (Plate 23), is
thought to have been executed in Rome and it represents a turning point in Botticelli's approach to the
subject and perhaps in his whole career. It is in many
respects the least 'Botticellian' and the most classical of
his Adorations. Significantly, it is probably the picture
Wölfflin had in mind when he spoke of Botticelli's
creation of 'a unified composition around one centre'.
Critics have often commented that the picture shows
the influence of Perugino and Signorelli whom Botticelli met while working in the Sistine Chapel. The
influence could have been through one specific composition, *The Nativity* fresco by Perugino which, until
Michelangelo obliterated it with his *Last Judgement*,
occupied the right-hand side of the altar wall of the
chapel (see diagram, p. 54). It is unlikely that Signorelli
arrived in Rome until after Botticelli and the other
artists left, so the suggestion of his influence can be
safely discounted. There is unfortunately no record of
the appearance of Perugino's composition, but it could
easily have been set in a landscape similar to the one in
Botticelli's picture and it might have had a 'stable' with
a heavy king-post roof on a row of sharply receding
columns like the one in the Washington *Adoration*.
Features of architecture and landscape related to this
Adoration occur in other pictures by Perugino.

Botticelli's classical 'Peruginesque' period lasted
throughout the 1480s and probably culminated in *The
Coronation of the Virgin* (Plate 15), after which the very
personal style of the *Divina Commedia* illustrations (Plates
70–73) and *The Mystic Nativity* (Plate IV) gradually
emerged. Although not illustrated in this book because
of their damaged and incomplete state, there exist
fragments of two further Adoration of the Magi

pictures which appear to be developments of the Washington composition and which are in the possession of the Soprintendenza alle Gallerie, Florence, the Pierpont Morgan Library, New York and the Fitzwilliam Museum, Cambridge, the last two being elements of one picture.

If it were possible to hang the Washington *Adoration of the Magi* next to the London *Mystic Nativity* viewers unfamiliar with the work of Botticelli might justifiably find it hard to believe that both pictures were by the same hand. The artist's latest style is most perfectly exemplified in *The Mystic Nativity* of 1500–01. The following passage was written by John Addington Symonds about Fra Angelico, but it translates into words a spirit so close to that of the late Botticelli, and *The Mystic Nativity* in particular, that I quote it in full: 'His world is a strange one—a world not of hills and fields and flowers and men of flesh and blood, but one where people are embodied ecstasies, the colours tints from evening clouds or apocalyptic jewels, the scenery a flood of light or a background of illuminated gold. His mystic gardens, where ransomed souls embrace, and dance with angels on the lawns outside the City of the Lamb, are such as were never trodden by the foot of man in any paradise of earth.' Botticelli may have been remembering Fra Angelico's *Last Judgement* in San Marco when he drew the foreground figures in *The Mystic Nativity*, and the dancing angels in the sky recall those in Rosellino's *Nativity* (fig. 9) but the style of the painting is outside most fifteenth-century terms of reference. He returned to the Gothic principle whereby the most important character in a composition was the largest in scale, and he abandoned modern architecture and scientific perspective in favour of a rural setting in which natural rock appears to have erupted from the shifting earth's crust in order to frame and protect the Holy Family. In many ways the picture is a synthesis of old and new in Botticelli's art. It is archaic in iconography and in the extensive use of gold, which underlies the whole of the thatch roof, the upper part of the sky and the dancing angels, but it is new in that it appears to have been executed in oil on canvas rather than Botticelli's usual tempera on panel, and in that it seems likely that it was painted purely as a vehicle for self-expression. The concept of 'art for art's sake' is more often associated with the sixteenth century and the Mannerist movement than with the late quattrocento, but the fact that *The Mystic Nativity* so unashamedly fails to meet the requirements of spatial realism and naturalism of an up-to-date picture of 1500 almost certainly precludes it from being a commission for public view.

A poignantly beautiful picture which is stylistically very close to *The Mystic Nativity* is the Granada *Agony in the Garden* (Plate 24), which was a commission but was destined for a site well away from the Florentine avant-garde. The composition differs little in essentials

fig. 12 Venetian, c. 1450
The Agony in the Garden
New York, Metropolitan Museum of Art
(Harris Brisbane Dick fund). Woodcut.

This is one of the scenes from Bonaventura's *Meditatione sopra la Passione*, printed in 1487, which re-used illustrations from the Venetian block-book, *Passion of Our Lord*, of c. 1450.

from an anonymous woodcut illustration of the same subject (fig. 12) made at least half a century earlier. Again Botticelli found the style of an earlier period more appropriate to his expressive need than that of his own time.

Also closely akin to *The Mystic Nativity* in its non-realistic approach is the illustrated *Divina Commedia* (Plates 70–73). Herbert Read in *The Art of Sculpture* wrote: 'The theory of perspective developed in the fifteenth century is a scientific convention; it is merely one way of describing space and has no absolute validity'. Botticelli treated the theory as if it had no validity whatsoever in the Dante drawings. Through the cantos of the *Inferno*, *Purgatorio* and *Paradiso* he turned art and the world upside down. In episode after episode fierce curling flames pour out of the ground and sometimes out of half-open tilted rhomboid tombs, and figures gnaw at each others' and their own flesh in a world of sharp-edged rocks, deep caverns and vicious thorny woods. Gradually, the scenes become calmer and emptier of figures, and Dante is transported into a state of purity and joy which is *Paradiso*.

The intensity of these drawings and the latest paintings is often associated with the puritanizing cult of Fra Girolamo Savonarola of San Marco whose emotional

fig. 13 Domenico GHIRLANDAIO
The Massacre of the Innocents
Florence, Church of Santa Maria Novella.
Fresco.

Ghirlandaio worked beside Botticelli in
Ognissanti and in the Sistine Chapel in Rome.
His fresco cycle in the choir of Santa Maria
Novella was completed in 1490.

rallying sermons finally led to political revolution and
his own execution in Florence in 1498. It is not entirely
clear how closely Botticelli was involved with the
monk's near-hysterical form of religion. Vasari claims
he became so ardent a follower that he gave up working
and spent his last years in poverty and distress, but one
of the few surviving documents concerning Botticelli's
old age does not endorse this view. In 1502 the agent of
the great patron of the arts Isabella d'Este, Marchioness
of Mantua, a demanding lady who did not take kindly
to emotional or capricious artists, wrote to his employer,
'Botticelli has been much extolled to me both as an
excellent painter and as a man who works willingly . . .'
This, written four years after Savonarola's death, does
not seem like a description of a man whose head was
turned by extremist religious fervour. Two years later
Botticelli was one of the committee chosen to decide on
a site for Michelangelo's *David*, which again indicates
that he must still have been regarded as a man of
stature in Florentine society.

One of the great qualities of Botticelli's *Divina
Commedia* illustrations is the clarity of the narrative. As
the scenes flow from page to page the forms of Dante
and Virgil can always be easily identified and their
gestures and expressions quickly interpreted. The experience of working in the Sistine Chapel (Plates V and
30–36), where Botticelli had the more difficult task of
being one of an artistic team creating a continuous
theme, must have sharpened his sense of narrative.
Some of his compositional arrangements in the Sistine
frescoes were indeed more successful in this respect than
those of other painters working in the chapel who, unlike Botticelli, had had the advantage of previous prac-
tice of fresco cycle painting. Agostino Taja's mid-
eighteenth-century guide to the Vatican singled out
Botticelli's *Punishment of the Rebels* (Plate V) as being
especially praiseworthy. In this painting, more than in
the other two which Botticelli painted for the Sistine
Chapel, the background and surrounding architecture
were manipulated to organize and punctuate the narrative. A centrally-placed arch is not an unusual feature
in fifteenth-century compositions, Gozzoli used one in
his *Jacob and Esau* which Botticelli could have seen in the
Camposanto at Pisa, but its effectiveness in *The Punishment of the Rebels* is striking and may have inspired
Ghirlandaio, one of the Sistine artists, when he painted
his *Massacre of the Innocents* (fig. 13) in Santa Maria
Novella.

Narrative is again the keynote of one of Botticelli's
small mythological paintings, *The 'Calumny' of Apelles*
(Plate 64) now in the Uffizi. The picture is literally

fig. 14 Baccio BALDINI
Pair of Dancers in a Wreath with Cupids
London, British Museum, Department of
Prints and Drawings. Engraving.

Vasari recounted that Baccio Baldini was the
engraver of Botticelli's designs for the 1481
edition of *La Divina Commedia* (Plates 70–73).
This *Pair of Dancers* of c. 1475 is one of the
'Otto Prints', a series of hunting and amorous
scenes intended to be pasted into gift boxes.

composed from two or more written descriptions of the
Calumny painted in the fourth century B.C. by the Greek
artist Apelles. Perhaps with this picture subconsciously
in his mind, Ruskin called Botticelli a 'reanimate
Greek', and even before *The 'Calumny' of Apelles* had
been painted a writer contemporary with Botticelli,
Ugolino Verino, had called him 'the successor of
Apelles'. Botticelli's connection with the Antique was
usually less direct than in *The 'Calumny' of Apelles* and is
generally far less easily understood. Although the
majority of scholars now agree on the identification of
the principal allegorical figures in *The Birth of Venus*
(Plate 66) and the *Primavera* (Plate 65), neither picture
illustrates an existing text as closely as *The 'Calumny'*
follows Lucian's and Alberti's description of Apelles's
painting.

The mythological pictures are set apart from the
Christian Adorations, Annunciations and Madonnas as
a result of the complexity and unfamiliarity of their
subject matter and because they reveal Botticelli as a
compositional innovator. Visual models for classical
themes were few and far between in the quattrocento.
Botticelli's solution was to adapt and transform suitable
existing images with such skill and artistry that he
appears to have created something absolutely new. No
obvious model for *Venus and Mars* (Plate 61) can be
found in panel painting of the period, but lovers are
sometimes depicted reclining opposite each other in

small scale decorative and engraved works of art, and
a seemingly insignificant detail such as the border of
Baccio Baldini's *Pair of Dancers* (fig. 14) could have been
the sort of image which provided the foundation for
Botticelli's composition. It is possible that some Flemish
tapestry may have inspired the strongly two-dimensional structure of the *Primavera* and, as Gombrich has
suggested, the traditional arrangement of the Baptism
of Christ may be the origin of the composition of his
Birth of Venus.

The three Graces of the *Primavera* are loosely based
on a classical sculpture group, such as one in the
Libreria Piccolomini, Siena, but unlike the classical
sculptor, and also unlike Raphael later on, Botticelli
chose to make his Graces move. They are usually said
to be dancing, but it might equally be said that their
bodies are simply infused with a spirit of movement.
Botticelli was not, as was Leonardo, interested in
dynamics, and he introduced movement as a means of
creating flowing linear compositions or as an expression
of narrative content, but never in the interest of depicting the muscularity of the human body in action.
Botticelli's figures are incapable of ever being entirely
static. This is demonstrated by the comparison of one
of Botticelli's 'still' figures, the St. John the Baptist of
The Bardi Altarpiece (Plate 9), with an earlier monumental depiction of the same saint in the same attitude
by Domenico Veneziano (fig. 15).

We know from the composition of *The 'Calumny' of
Apelles* that Botticelli had read Alberti's *De Pictura*. This
treatise also contains some advice on movement which
is graphically reflected in the *Primavera* and *The Birth
of Venus*: 'it will be a good idea, when we wish clothing
to have movement, to have in the corner of the picture
the face of the West or South wind blowing between
clouds and moving all the clothing before it. The pleas-
ing result will be that those sides of the bodies the wind
strikes will appear under the covering of the clothes almost as if they were naked, since the clothes are made
to adhere to the body by the force of the wind . . .'
On hair Alberti wrote, 'let it twist around as if to tie
itself in a knot, and wave upwards in the air like flames,
let it weave beneath other hair and sometimes lift on
one side and another'. The hair of Venus in *The Birth
of Venus* was created almost as if by Alberti's command.

Although the words of Alberti on movement fit
Botticelli's images so well that we cannot fail to associate the two, the artist never allowed himself to be
bound by rules. Unpredictability is a characteristic of
his art. In *La Divina Commedia, Inferno*, Canto XXXII
Botticelli drew Dante with two heads in order to ex-
press the turning movement which follows the shifting
of the poet's attention from one subject to another. The
lack of respect for accepted artistic convention which
Botticelli displayed on occasion can easily confuse the
historian whose job it is to unravel the meaning of the
images. The two-headed Dante is unlikely to be mis-

fig. 15 Domenico VENEZIANO
Madonna and Child with Saints, detail of
St. John
Florence, Galleria degli Uffizi. Tempera on
panel.
The picture was painted for the Church of
Santa Lucia de' Magnoli in Florence in the
mid-1440s. It is often referred to as *The St.
Lucy Altarpiece*.

fig. 16 Miniature figures of Botticelli's *Venus*,
cast in alabaster powder or some other com-
pound, are found not only in Italian gift
shops. In a shop in Kent they jostle with
Rodin's *The Kiss* and the *Venus de Milo*.

understood in the context of a series, but in the large
mythological paintings, which have no continuous
narrative content, the borderline between what is
meant to be pure representation and what is 'artistic
licence' is more subtle. In *The Birth of Venus* the two
figures flying in from the left propelling Venus towards
the shore are usually taken to be zephyrs, but the author
of a fairly recent reappraisal of the picture calls the

female figure Chloris, the earth nymph, because in his
opinion she is not blowing and has no wings. In fact it
is clear from the original picture that a stream of breath
or wind is issuing from her lips and she *does* have wings.
There are four wings behind the entwined figures, and
although the two wings behind the woman do not
appear to be attached to her anatomically correctly,
why should something that is in essence 'unreal', as
figures do not have wings, be painted in a 'real' way?
Botticelli no doubt felt that it was quite sufficient to
state that four wings shared out between two people
meant two wings each. This kind of visual shorthand
is carried right through *The Birth of Venus*. The waves
from which Venus has risen are, as Yashiro, the most
inspired of Botticelli's biographers, observed, 'as unreal
as they can be'. They appear as a pattern of white 'V'
shapes on a flat ground of light greenish-blue which
makes little attempt to suggest the transparency and
wetness of water. The tree trunks too, on the right, are
stiff brown columns which are more akin to architecture than to nature, and their unreality is heightened,
as if that were necessary, by a strip of gold applied in
short regular strokes down one side of each trunk.

The combination of esoteric subject matter and bold
and fluent design which caused certain nineteenth-
century authors to shy away from *The Birth of Venus* also
made the picture, conversely, one of the most popular
images in Italian art in the twentieth century. In
Crowe and Cavalcaselle's *History of Italian Painting*
(1911) the only comment on the style of the painting is
'The figures are a little out of balance'. Today the figure
of Venus in particular is so well loved that it has even
been translated into three-dimensional form for mass
sale in Britain and abroad (fig. 16) and is so familiar
that a large proportion of the viewers of BBC television's
Monty Python's Flying Circus could be expected to recog-
nize her when, seen on the screen as a cut-out with
articulated legs, she performed a variation of the
Charleston on the edge of her shell. *The Birth of Venus*
above all other of Botticelli's paintings has 'stage
presence'. Kenneth Clark recalls its dramatic entrance
to the famous 1930 exhibition of Italian art at Burlington House, London. 'With my love of *coups de théâtre* I
asked the Academy attendants to keep Botticelli's
Birth of Venus on one side until I could collect everyone
working on the hanging to watch her rise from the
basement into the gallery; and it was an unforgettable
moment.' Lord Clark had seen the picture many times
before, but viewing it in different surroundings and,
literally, from an unusual angle, he experienced its
impact anew. For those of us who have to make a fresh
presentation of Botticelli's pictures in words and photographs alone the task is more difficult. We can only ask,
as Walter Pater did in 1870, 'What is the peculiar
sensation, what is the peculiar quality of pleasure,
which his work has the property of exciting in us, and
which we cannot get elsewhere?'

VILLA DI CASTELLO (21) (23) (24) (p)

VILLA LEMMI (10)

S. BARNABA (4) (15)

S. MARCO (5)

Via Panicale Via Guelfa

Orti Oricellari

(i) (j) PALAZZO MEDICI (k) (l) (m) (n)

Via degli

Via della Scala

S. MARTINO DELLA SCALA (f)

S. MARIA NOVELLA (6) (t)

13

CASA PUCCI

(11) (12) CASA VESPUCCI

Via Palazzuolo

Borgo Ognissanti

PISA CATHEDRAL (a)

(9) OGNISSANTI

Via del Porcellana

S. PAOLINO (19)

S. MARIA MAGGIORE (2) (20)

Via de' Tornabuoni

S. MARIA DEL FIORE (h)

1

17 (c)

d (e)

S. MARIA DI MONTICELLI (o)

ORSAN MICHELE (s)

Piazza della Signoria

PALAZZO DELLA SIGNORIA

BOTTICELLI'S HOUSE

VILLA DELLO SPEDALETTO (g)

Ponte Vecchio

S. SPIRITO (3)

Via dei Bardi

S. ELIZABETTA DELLE CONVERTITE

Via del Campuccio

Piazza de' Pitti

(b)

Via Romana

S. PIER GATTOLINO (r)

FLORENCE
THE LOCATION OF
BOTTICELLI'S WORKS
IN THE 15th CENTURY

ROME (7) (8)

Chronology

Documented Events	Approximate Chronological Sequence of Pictures
1445	Birth of Alessandro Filipepi, later known as Botticelli, in Florence.	
1467	Filippo Lippi left Florence for Spoleto; Botticelli is believed to have been in his workshop before this date.	
1467–70		*Madonna and Child in a Mandorla of Seraphim* (Plate 1); *Madonna and Child in an Archway* (Plate 2); *Madonna and Child with Two Angels* (Plate 3); *The Adoration of the Magi* (Plate 17)
1470	The Pollaiuolo brothers and Botticelli painted *Virtues* for the hall of the Arte della Mercanzia.	*Fortitude* (Plate 6); *The Finding of the Dead Holofernes* (Plate 54); *The Return of Judith* (Plate 55); *Madonna and Child with an Angel with Symbols of the Eucharist* (Plate 4)
1472	Filippino Lippi was working as an assistant to Botticelli.	*Madonna and Child Enthroned with Six Saints* (Plate 8); *The Adoration of the Magi* (Plate III)
1474	Botticelli went to Pisa (27 January).	*St. Sebastian* (Plate 7); *The Adoration of the Magi* (Plate 21); *The Raczinsky Tondo* (Plate 50)
1478	The Pazzi conspiracy (26 April); Botticelli commissioned to portray the hanged criminals in fresco on the wall of the Palazzo Vecchio.	*Primavera* (Plate 65); *Abundance* (Plate 69); *St. Augustine* (Plate 37); *The Annunciation* (Plate 56)
1481–82	Botticelli worked in Rome.	The Sistine Chapel frescoes (Plates V and 30–36); *The Adoration of the Magi* (Plate 23); the Villa Lemmi frescoes (Plates 39 and 40); *The Birth of Venus* (Plate 66)
1483–84	Botticelli worked at the Medici Villa dello Spedaletto near Volterra on decorative frescoes.	*Portrait of a Young Man* (Plate 25); *Portrait of Giuliano de' Medici* (Plate 28); *Portrait of a Young Man Holding a Medallion* (Plate 27); *The Story of Nastagio degli Onesti* (Plate 49); *Pallas and the Centaur* (Plate 63)

1485	....	*The Bardi Altarpiece* (Plate 9); *Madonna of the Magnificat* (Plate 51); *Madonna and Child with a Book* (Plate 5)
1487	....	*Madonna of the Pomegranate* (Plate 52); *Portrait of a Man with a Medal* (Plate 26); *Portrait of Lorenzo Lorenzano* (Plate 29); *Venus and Mars* (Plate 61); *The San Barnaba Altarpiece* (Plate 10); *The Annunciation* (Plate 57)
1490	....	*The Coronation of the Virgin* (Plate 15); *Pietà* (Plate 58); *The Panciatichi Pietà* (Plate 59)
1491	Botticelli commissioned (18 May) to decorate vault of the Chapel of St. Zenobius in Santa Maria del Fiore (his share of the work never completed); Botticelli acted as member of the committee to consider designs for façade of Santa Maria del Fiore.	*Three Angels* (Plate 68); '*Noli me Tangere*' (Plate 43); *The 'Calumny' of Apelles* (Plate 64); '*La Derelicta*' (Plate 38); *The Communion of St. Jerome* (Plate 44); *St. Augustine in his Cell* (Plate VI); *Madonna and Child with Three Angels* (Plate 53)
1496	Botticelli painted a fresco of St. Francis in the dormitory of Santa Maria di Monticelli (the building destroyed 1529–30).	*Scenes from the Life of St. Zenobius* (Plates 45–48); *Pentecost* (Plate 60)
1497	Botticelli and assistants commissioned to paint decorative frescoes for the Medici Villa di Castello.	
1497–1500		*The Annunciation* (Plate VII)
1500	....	*The Mystic Nativity* (Plate IV); *The Agony in the Garden* (Plate 24); *The Story of Virginia* (Plate 41); *The Story of Lucretia* (Plate 42); the *Divina Commedia* illustrations (Plates 70–73)
1504	Botticelli acted as member of the committee to decide on placing of Michelangelo's *David*.	
1510	Death of Botticelli; buried in Ognissanti (17 May).	

Bibliography

The giant monograph by Herbert P. Horne, *Alessandro Filipepi, commonly called Sandro Botticelli* (London 1908) is irreplaceable. It is painstakingly researched and quotes documents in full, including the relevant text of the Anonimo Gaddiano, originally written c. 1542–48, and both editions of Vasari's *Life of Botticelli* (1550 and 1568). Yukio Yashiro's *Sandro Botticelli and the Florentine Renaissance* (London 1929) is more passionately written and contains a useful chronology and extensive bibliography. For quick reference Roberto Salvini, *Tutta la pittura del Botticelli*, 2 vols. (Milan 1958) and *The Complete Paintings of Botticelli*, introduction by Michael Levey and with notes and catalogue by Gabriele Mandel (English edition, London 1970), are both easy to use. The most recent publications are L. D. and Helen S. Ettlinger, *Botticelli* (London 1976), Kenneth Clark, *The Drawings by Sandro Botticelli for Dante's 'Divine Comedy'* (London 1976) and a new monograph by Ronald Lightbown, *Botticelli* (London 1977). Of all the museum and gallery catalogues containing works by Botticelli, Martin Davies's *National Gallery: The Earlier Italian Schools* (2nd edition, London 1961) remains the most informative.

Rather than attempt to give a definitive bibliography which could cover several pages, I list here sources which have been quoted in my text and in general those books or articles which, in addition to the ones cited above, have proved most useful in the compilation of this book.

Francesco Albertini, *Memoriale di Molte Statue et Picture di Florentia* (Florence 1510) reprinted in *Gregg International Publishers' Five Early Guides to Rome and Florence* (Farnborough 1972).

Aldo Bertini, *Drawings by Botticelli* (New York 1968).

Francesco Bocchi, *Bellezze della Città di Firenze* (Florence 1591) and the Giovanni Cinelli edition of 1677.

P. Cannon-Brookes, 'Botticelli's "Pentecost", An Interpretation', *Apollo* (1962).

Julia Cartwright, *Sandro Botticelli* (London 1903).

J. A. Crowe and G. B. Cavalcaselle, *The History of Italian Painting* (Langton Douglas edition in English) (London 1911).

Kenneth Clark, *Another Part of the Wood* (London 1974).

C. Dempsey, 'Botticelli's Three Graces', *The Journal of the Warburg and Courtauld Institutes* (1971).

C. Dempsey, 'Mercurius Ver: The Sources of Botticelli's "Primavera" ', *The Journal of the Warburg and Courtauld Institutes* (1968).

L. D. Ettlinger, *The Sistine Chapel before Michelangelo* (Oxford 1965).

E. H. Gombrich, 'Apollonio di Giovanni', *The Journal of the Warburg and Courtauld Institutes* (1955).

E. H. Gombrich, 'Botticelli's Mythologies', *The Journal of the Warburg and Courtauld Institutes* (1945).

C. Grayson, *Leon Battista Alberti: On Painting and On Sculpture* (London 1972).

Martin Kemp, 'Botticelli's Glasgow "Annunciation": Patterns of Instability', *The Burlington Magazine* (1977).

Michael Levey, 'Botticelli and 19th century England', *The Journal of the Warburg and Courtauld Institutes* (1960).

Michael Levey, *Themes and Painters in the National Gallery Number 11: Botticelli* (London 1974).

F. Lippmann, *Drawings by Sandro Botticelli for Dante's 'Divina Commedia'* (London 1896).

M. Meiss, *The Great Age of Fresco* (London 1970).

W. and E. Paatz, *Die Kirchen von Florenz* (Frankfurt-am-Main 1955).

J. G. Phillips, *Early Florentine Designers and Engravers* (Cambridge, Massachusetts 1955).

H. Ruhemann, 'Technical Analysis of an Early Painting by Botticelli', *Studies in Conservation* (1955).

John A. Symonds, *Renaissance in Italy, The Fine Arts* (London 1877).

Agostino Taja, *Descrizione del Palazzo Apostolico Vaticano* (Rome 1750).

G. F. Waagen, *Works of Art and Artists in England* (London 1838).

H. Wölfflin, *Classic Art* (first published 1899; English edition, London 1952).

F. Zeri, *La Galleria Pallavicini in Roma* (Florence 1959).

Note to the Plates

All except one of Botticelli's paintings illustrated here are described as in tempera, that is, pigment suspended in an aqueous medium, usually egg. Where technical examinations of paintings have been made, notably in the case of the London *Adoration of the Magi* (Plate 17), it has been shown that the paintings also contain oil and oil and resin glazes carrying either dissolved dyestuffs, such as madder, or particles of pigment. The panel is probably poplar in most cases but only very rarely is the wood-type specified in museum catalogues.

(opposite)
I *Primavera* (detail of Plate 65)
(overleaf)
II *The Birth of Venus* (see Plate 66)

(above left)

1 *Madonna and Child in a Mandorla of Seraphim*

FLORENCE, Galleria degli Uffizi. Tempera on panel 120 × 65 cm. Original frame. Suffering from rubbing, losses in areas of gilding and a coating of discoloured varnish.

The early history of the panel is unknown, but it was recorded without an attribution in a Uffizi inventory of 1784. In 1893 it was published in Ulmann's *Sandro Botticelli*, since when it has been accepted as one of the artist's earliest works, painted before the *Fortitude* (Plate 6) which is known to have been finished by August 1470. Diffidently composed, carefully excluding the complexities of spatial description, this picture nevertheless incorporates in embryonic form many of the stylistic idiosyncrasies of Botticelli's mature work. The oversize Child, for example, reappears only slightly refined in *The San Barnaba Altarpiece* (Plate 10) of at least twelve years later, and the uncomfortably long arm of the Madonna is resolved as a graceful and positive feature of the design in such figures as the Venus of *The Birth of Venus* (Plate 66).

(above right)

2 *Madonna and Child in an Archway* (*Madonna del Roseto*)

FLORENCE, Galleria degli Uffizi. Tempera on panel 124 × 64 cm.

This panel hung in the old Camera di Commercio on the east side of the Piazza della Signoria before it was moved to the Uffizi in the eighteenth century. Its original location is unknown. It is a far more confident painting than the *Madonna and Child in a Mandorla of Seraphim* (Plate 1), and despite the fact that Morelli, in 1897, judged it a 'bastarda opera', most authors agree in attributing it to Botticelli and the period of the *Fortitude* (Plate 6), around 1470.

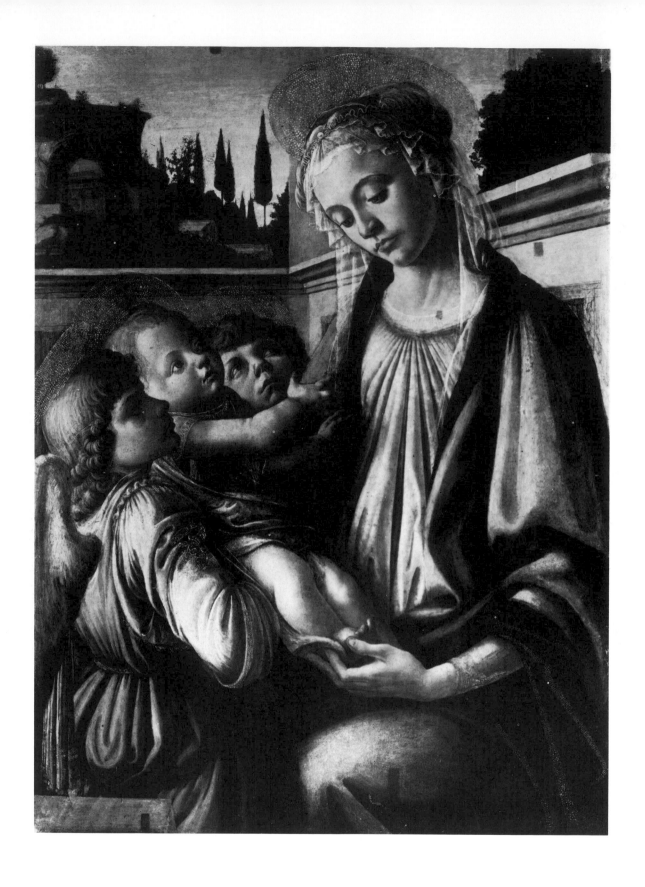

3 *Madonna and Child with Two Angels*
NAPLES, Gallerie Nazionale di Capodimonte. Tempera on panel 100 × 71 cm. Almost entirely repainted until restoration in 1957.

This *Madonna* was first recorded in 1697 in the Palazzo Farnese, Rome, attributed to Filippino Lippi. The image of two angels presenting Christ to his mother was derived from Filippo Lippi and is best known in his *Madonna Adoring the Divine Child* of 1457 in the Uffizi. Although this picture by Botticelli still belongs to his earliest period of 1468–70, a degree of finesse in the treatment of draperies is already present. The Madonna's transparent veil provides a foretaste of the dazzling brushwork which later clothes the Graces in the *Primavera* (Plate 65).

4 *Madonna and Child with an Angel with Symbols of the Eucharist* (*Madonna dell' Eucharista*)
BOSTON, Isabella Stewart Gardner Museum. Tempera on panel 85 × 64·5 cm.

The composition of grapes and ears of wheat which the Child is blessing allude to the wine and bread of Communion. In the collection of the Principe Chigi, duca d'Ariccia, by the eighteenth century, this painting was sold in 1899 to Edmund Despretz. In the same year it was bought by Mrs. Gardner through Berenson from Colnaghi in London. It arrived in Boston in 1901 after being exhibited in London. Sir Charles Eastlake recorded in his *Notebook I* of 1856 that he saw this *Madonna and Child*, a 'good composition', in the Palazzo Chigi, Rome, attributed to Ghirlandaio. Although he had difficulty judging its quality through the grime which then coated its surface, he considered it to be by Filippino Lippi or Botticelli. It is generally stated that Morelli confirmed in 1891 the 'traditional' attribution to Botticelli, but if Eastlake's notes are correct this tradition cannot have dated back earlier than 1856. It is quite possible that Eastlake was the first to propose the Botticelli attribution. The panel may date from the period immediately after the *Fortitude* (Plate 6) when Botticelli, as evidenced by the facial types, was still under the influence of Pollaiuolo and Verrocchio.

5 *Madonna and Child with a Book* (*Madonna del Libro*)
MILAN, Museo Poldi-Pezzoli. Tempera on panel 58 × 39·5 cm. Heavy overpainting removed in restoration of 1951.

For clarity of composition and tenderness of expression this *Madonna* of the 1480s is unsurpassed in Botticelli's *oeuvre*. It was first catalogued in the Poldi-Pezzoli collection as a work of Botticelli in 1881, and since then most scholars have recognized its connection, both in terms of style and technique, with the *Madonna of the Magnificat* (Plate 51).

6 *Fortitude*

FLORENCE, Galleria degli Uffizi. Tempera on panel
167 × 87 cm.

Botticelli was paid in August 1470 for the *Fortitude* which
hung originally with six other *Virtues* by the Pollaiuolo
brothers in the hall of the Arte della Mercanzia in the
Piazza della Signoria, where magistrates sat for cases
arising from commercial transactions. Although it was
perhaps not immediately obvious to onlookers in the
magistrates' chamber that this graceful figure was intended
to epitomize strength and courage, they must have
admired the luxuriant architecture of the throne and the
glittering costume. Cavalcaselle, in 1894, was not,
however, impressed. He complained that the *Fortitude*
simply followed the other *Virtues* and shared 'Their
energy of movement, vulgarity of type and coarseness of
extremities and articulations'.

7 *St. Sebastian*

BERLIN (Dahlem), Staatliche Gemäldegalerie. Tempera on
panel 195 × 75 cm. Panel damaged at edges, particularly
on the right.

According to the Anonimo Gaddiano this picture was
hung on a pillar in the Church of Santa Maria Maggiore
on 20 January 1474. It had gone from the church by the
seventeenth century, and its history is unknown until it
was acquired by the Berlin Museum with the Solly
collection in 1821, attributed to Pollaiuolo. Unlike
Mantegna, Tura, Antonello da Messina, Pollaiuolo and
the majority of other fifteenth-century artists who painted
St. Sebastian, Botticelli did not seize on the legend that
the saint was a member of the Roman Imperial Guard
and accordingly embellish his scene with ostentatious
classical paraphernalia. Instead, his backdrop to the figure
is a sunny landscape with a strange little turreted
harbour in the distance. There is a small but significant
reference to militarism in the cavalcade of soldiers in the
middle distance. One of the figures has just paused and
shot an arrow right through a bird which plummets from
the sky to its death. Botticelli perhaps intended this
background incident to underline the central theme of
the picture.

8 *Madonna and Child Enthroned with Six Saints*
FLORENCE, Galleria degli Uffizi. Tempera on panel 170 × 194 cm. Much sixteenth-century
repainting, especially in areas of Madonna and Child and two foreground saints.

After being moved from the Church of Sant' Ambrogio, Piazza Sant' Ambrogio, to the Accademia,
this picture came to rest in the Uffizi in 1946. Early sources record a panel by Botticelli in the
Church of the Augustinian nuns of Santa Elizabetta delle Convertite not far from the Palazzo Pitti,
a foundation for repentant prostitutes. A number of scholars have associated this altarpiece with the
lost panel, but with the exception of Mary Magdalen on the left, the other saints, John the Baptist,
Francis, Catherine and the Medici patrons Cosmas and Damian have no obvious relevance to the
mission of the nuns of Santa Elizabetta. The faces of the two outermost female saints are the only
ones to have escaped overpainting, and they suggest a date close to the *Madonna and Child with
Symbols of the Eucharist* (Plate 4) in which the Child is posed similarly.

9 *The Bardi Altarpiece*
BERLIN (Dahlem), Staatliche Gemäldegalerie. Tempera on panel 185 × 180 cm.

The Bardi Altarpiece is Botticelli's most immaculately finished picture. It was commissioned by Giovanni d'Agnolo de' Bardi in 1484–85 for his family chapel, the first on the left on the end wall of the chancel of Santo Spirito, now occupied by a gloomy *St. Clare Communicates before Christ* by the seventeenth-century painter Vignali. Botticelli received a final payment on 3 August 1485 of seventy-eight florins for the altarpiece. Earlier, on 7 February, Giuliano da Sangallo had received twenty-four florins for carving the frame which is unfortunately lost without trace. Sangallo later designed the sacristy of Santo Spirito, which was begun in 1488. The picture shows the two name saints of the donor, John the Baptist, on the left, and John the Evangelist. The marble bench-style throne in the picture recalls the seat on which Filippo Lippi placed his *Seven Saints*, in the National Gallery, London. Botticelli may have learnt from Lippi not to have qualms about applying more than one eye level to a composition. Here the four tall lily vases are seen from below, yet the top ledge of the throne on which they stand is seen from above.

10 *The San Barnaba Altarpiece*

FLORENCE, Galleria degli Uffizi. Tempera on panel 268 × 280 cm. Cut at top edge; enlarged at top and base by Agostino Veracini in 1717, additions removed after 1919; damage to centre vertical join in panel affects faces of Madonna and Child.

The full extent of Albertini's entry for San Barnaba in his guide to Florence of 1510 reads 'In S. Barnaba there is a large altarpiece by Sandro Botticelli, and other pictures.' The painting was commissioned around 1488–90 by the Guild of Medici e Speziali, patrons of the Church of San Barnaba. It originally decorated the high altar, but by the time of Cinelli's edition of Bocchi's *Belleze di Firenze* (1677) it had been moved behind the altar. The date of this move is sometimes erroneously given as 1700. When the monastery and church were suppressed in 1808 the altarpiece was placed in the Accademia and was transferred from there to the Uffizi in 1919. As in *The Bardi Altarpiece* (Plate 9) Botticelli chose a rich red as the predominant hue and took pains to embellish the composition with a magnificent variety of surfaces and textures. The saints are, from the left, Catherine of Alexandria, Augustine, Barnabas (with raised hand), John the Baptist, Ignatius and Michael.

12 *The San Barnaba Altarpiece*
(detail of Plate 10).

13 *The Vision of St. Augustine*, predella panel of *The San Barnaba Altarpiece* (Plate 10)
FLORENCE, Galleria degli Uffizi. Tempera on panel 20 × 38 cm.

Although the absence of any record of the original frame of *The San Barnaba Altarpiece* prevents an accurate reconstruction of the predella, the width of the picture and its composition suggests that there were seven separate panels. Of these four survive, all in the Uffizi. They depict *The Vision of St. Augustine*, to correspond with the figure of St. Augustine, second from the left in the main panel, a *Pietà* for the centre piece, *Salome with the Head of the Baptist*, to be placed beneath St. John, third from the right, and *The Removal of the Heart of St. Ignatius*, positioned below the grey-bearded St. Ignatius, second from the right. St. Augustine, while meditating and trying to fathom the mystery of the Trinity, saw in a vision a child whose wish was to transfer the sea into one small hole. When Augustine told him this was impossible the child replied that it was no more futile than the saint's efforts to transfer the great mystery of the Trinity into his small brain.

(*opposite*)
15 *The Coronation of the Virgin*
FLORENCE, Galleria degli Uffizi. Tempera on panel 378 × 258 cm.

The Guild of Goldsmiths commissioned the picture between 1488 and 1490 for their Chapel of Sant' Alo on the left of the main door of the Church of San Marco. It was moved in 1596 to the Chapter of San Marco and then in 1807 to the Accademia. In 1919 it was transferred to the Uffizi. It is the only altarpiece by Botticelli to have retained its predella intact. As with *The San Barnaba Altarpiece* (Plates 10 and 13) the predella reflects incidents from the lives of the principal saints in the main composition, John the Evangelist, the Church Fathers Augustine and Jerome and the patron of goldsmiths, Eligius, familiar in Florentine art through the figure by Nanni di Banco on the west side of Or San Michele. *The Coronation of the Virgin* is the most grandiose and formal of Botticelli's altar panels. In critical history it has appealed to those who have found his art lacking in compositional structure. Cavalcaselle, for example, proclaimed almost with a sigh of relief that in this picture Botticelli 'succeeds in realizing at last the idea of infinity and space'.

14 *Sacred Scenes*, predella of *The Coronation of the Virgin* (Plate 15)
FLORENCE, Galleria degli Uffizi. Tempera on panel 21 × 269 cm.

The original frame in which the predella was set does not survive. The scenes represented are *St. John on the Island of Patmos*, *St. Augustine in his Study*, *The Annunciation*, *St. Jerome in the Desert* and *St. Eligius in his Workshop*, about to restore a foreleg to a horse and a nose to a lady. The last scene is related to a relief of the same subject by Nanni di Banco below his *St. Eligius* on the exterior of Or San Michele.

17 *The Adoration of the Magi*

LONDON, National Gallery. Tempera on panel 50 × 136 cm. Two 2 cm. strips of paint added later at the left and right edges; restored 1940.

This is Botticelli's smallest and earliest *Adoration*. Its original home is unknown but it was in the Lombardi-Baldi collection, Florence, by 1845, and before that was in the possession of the Marchese Ippolito Orlandini of Florence. Eastlake purchased the picture with other items from the Lombardi-Baldi collection in 1857. It appears to date from before 1470. The numerous *pentimenti* and changes of technique have long puzzled scholars and even the detailed technical analysis made at the National Gallery after the picture was restored has far from settled the question of whether a second hand was responsible for some areas or whether Botticelli re-worked some of the figures himself at a later date. The scientific investigation did reveal that although the painting technique is in many respects experimental and varies from one group of figures to the next, it is at the same time highly skilful and inventive. The forms are built up in many successive layers of translucent pigment. The sleeve of the second kneeling king, for instance, is composed of no less than six layers of paint, some of which consist of pigment in a tempera medium and others of dyestuffs dissolved in an oil glaze. On the rough back of the panel are a drawing of a female figure holding a shield, part of a face and other scribbles, all possibly by Botticelli.

(*opposite*)
16 *The Coronation of The Virgin* (detail of Plate 15)

In order to distinguish the heavenly from the earthly realms below, Botticelli brought back the seraphim of the earliest *Madonna* in the Uffizi (Plate 1) and added a semi-circle of dancing angels which looks forward to *The Mystic Nativity* (Plate IV). In a letter of 1876, the painter Edward Burne-Jones, yearning for another glimpse of this picture wrote, 'At the back of the Virgin the rays of gold rain on a most dear face that looks up and I want to see it . . .'

18 *The Adoration of the Magi* (detail of Plate 17)

(*opposite*)
III *The Adoration of the Magi*
LONDON, National Gallery. Tempera on panel (tondo) 131·5 cm. diameter. Slightly rubbed; restored 1956.

The picture may be the one mentioned as being in the Casa Pucci, Florence by Vasari in the 1568 edition of his *Vite*. It was still in Florence, in the Palazzo Guicciardini in 1807. After passing through the Dubois and Coningham collections it was recorded by Waagen as a work of Filippo Lippi in the Fuller Maitland collection at Stansted House, Essex in 1854. Morelli recognized the picture as by Botticelli, but as Horne observed, the National Gallery authorities 'thought fit to attribute it to Filippino Lippi' after acquiring it in 1878 from Fuller Maitland for £800. In the same year the National Gallery also bought *The Mystic Nativity* (Plate IV) from him for £1500. Although this *Adoration* is still an early picture it is one of Botticelli's most ingeniously structured compositions. The Virgin, set at the exact centre of the circle, is posed in the same way as she is in *The San Barnaba Altarpiece* (Plate 10) of at least fourteen years later. Also, as in the San Barnaba picture, her importance is emphasized by the architectural elements which surround and frame her, although in *The Adoration* arched classical ruins take the place of the interior church setting of the later *sacra conversazione* composition. There is even in this *Adoration* an echo of the inverted shell often found in formal interior groups as part of the architecture above the Virgin's throne. A similar semi-circular shape appears as a patch of sky seen through the furthest arch above and behind the Madonna and Child. The oversize peacock, which can also be seen in the Lippi *Adoration* (fig. 10) in Washington and, rather smaller, in Botticelli's Uffizi *Adoration* (Plate 21), was probably intended to symbolize resurrection and immortality, as the flesh of the peacock was supposed to be immune to decay and this belief gave rise to the association of the bird with immortal life in both pagan and Christian iconography. The use of a resurrection symbol in connection with the infant Christ is not unusual; the pomegranate in the *Madonna of the Pomegranate* (Plate 52) has the same connotation. As in the early rectangular *Adoration* (Plate 17) a number of *pentimenti* are visible in this tondo, especially in the sky where the architecture once continued across to the right edge.

19 *The Mystic Nativity* (X-ray photograph detail of Plate IV)

At the age of sixty-five and after over thirty years of experience Botticelli was still able to accept that the first marks he made with his brush were not always the right ones. In the course of painting the figure of St. Joseph he completely changed the position of his right foot.

(*opposite*)
IV *The Mystic Nativity*
LONDON, National Gallery. Oil (?) on canvas 108·5 × 75 cm. Slightly damaged by flaking and wearing; restored 1958.

Like the tondo *Adoration* (Plate III) *The Mystic Nativity* was purchased by the National Gallery from the Fuller Maitland collection, Stansted House, Essex in 1878. Fuller Maitland acquired it from Smith (1847) and before that it had been with Brown and in the Ottley collection, London. Ottley bought the picture from the Villa Aldobrandini in Rome, probably in the 1790s. It was the first picture by Botticelli to arrive in England correctly attributed, perhaps simply because it is the only one to be signed and dated. *The Times* of 2 October 1878, announcing the National Gallery's acquisition of *The Mystic Nativity*, described the dancing angelic host as 'unquestionably the supreme expression of Botticelli's genius—one might almost say an invention unsurpassed in the whole range of art'. The signature is incorporated in the Greek inscription at the top of the picture: 'I Sandro painted this picture at the end of the year 1500 [?] in the troubles of Italy in the half time after the time according to the XIth chapter of St. John in the second woe of the Apocalypse in the loosing of the devil for three and a half years then he will be chained in the XIIth chapter and we shall see clearly [?] . . . as in this picture'. The date is almost certainly intended to be the end of the year 1500. Much of the meaning of the inscriptions and images in this picture is obscure. The unusual feature of angels embracing three men holding and crowned with olive branches must be intended to illustrate Luke II : 14, 'Glory to God in the highest and peace, good will among men', a passage which is inscribed in Latin on the scrolls carried by the angels in the sky above. At the coming of Christ and the consequent good will among men, symbolized by the embracing figures, several devils are trying to hide themselves in fissures in the ground. It is not clear, however, in what way Botticelli meant them to relate to the apocalyptic passage referred to in the Greek inscription at the top of the picture. The reference is, in fact, not even accurate: the devil is not chained in the twelfth chapter of Revelation but in the twentieth. The 'troubles' have been variously interpreted as the disturbances in Florence following the death of Savonarola in 1498, the French invasion of northern Italy in 1499 or Cesare Borgia's invasion of the Romagna in the same year.

21 *The Adoration of the Magi*
FLORENCE, Galleria degli Uffizi. Tempera on panel 111 × 134 cm. Scattered areas of discoloured retouching now visible.

The Uffizi picture is the only surviving *Adoration* for which early documentation exists. Vasari described how it hung above an altar between the two west doors of Santa Maria Novella, on the left as one entered the church by the centre door. It was commissioned around 1475–77 by Giovanni Lami of the Guild of Moneychangers, a close associate of the Medici. The patronage of the altar descended to the Fedini family and to a Spanish merchant, Mandragoni, who in turn sold the patronage of the altar to Bernardo Vecchietti who replaced Botticelli's *Adoration* with an *Annunciation* by Santi di Tito. *The Adoration* reappeared in the Medici Villa of Poggio Imperiale and was transferred to the Uffizi in 1796, attributed to Ghirlandaio. Vasari, who had a personal interest in the picture, having been employed by Mandragoni to refashion the altar surround, pointed out that the main figures of the kings and bystanders are portraits of the Medici. The king kneeling to kiss Christ's foot is Cosimo de' Medici and the other two kneeling kings his sons Piero, with the ermine gown, and Giovanni. Piero's sons Lorenzo 'il Magnifico' and Giuliano are believed to be the young man furthest left and the dark haired figure with downcast eyes, seen in profile to the front of the right hand group. A number of scholars have been tempted to identify the handsome man on the extreme right, looking out of the picture, as Botticelli himself.

(opposite)
20 *The Mystic Nativity* (detail of Plate IV)

23 *The Adoration of the Magi*
WASHINGTON, National Gallery of Art (Mellon collection). Tempera on panel 70·2 × 104·2 cm.

A French engraver, Perallis, is thought to have acquired the picture in Rome and from him it entered The Hermitage, St. Petersburg, in 1808 as a work of Mantegna. It was recognized as a Botticelli by Waagen in 1864. After being sold in 1933 it entered the Andrew W. Mellon collection in 1937. It is usually believed to be the *Adoration* which the Anonimo Gaddiano mentioned that Botticelli painted while he was in Rome between 1481 and 1482 working in the Sistine Chapel (Plates V and 30–36). Once again architecture is used to demonstrate the central importance of the Madonna, but in this panel the actual centre of the painted area is somewhat to the right of the Virgin.

(*opposite*)
22 *The Adoration of the Magi* (detail of Plate 21)

24 *The Agony in the Garden*

GRANADA, Capilla Real. Tempera (?) on panel
53 × 35 cm.

Probably the first work by Botticelli to leave Italy *The
Agony in the Garden* was listed among the works of art
which Isabella I, 'the Catholic', Queen of Castile,
commissioned, not long before her death in 1504, to
decorate the Capilla Real in Granada. Stylistically the
picture is very closely related to *The Mystic Nativity*
(Plate IV), though it is only about half as large. The
sleeping figure of St. Peter on the left only has to turn his
head to become the St. Joseph of *The Mystic Nativity*, and
the olive branches carried by angels in *The Mystic
Nativity* could well have been plucked from the trees
which surround Christ in the Garden of Gethsemane.
This poignant and beautiful picture has received scant
attention in the literature presumably because it happens
to be in Spain, rather than because it is in any way
unworthy of the artist.

(*opposite*)
25 *Portrait of a Young Man*

LONDON, National Gallery. Tempera on panel 37·5 × 28·2 cm. Cleaned 1968.

Sold as a self portrait by Masaccio at the Colonel Matthew Smith sale, 12 May 1804, to Northwick, the picture was subsequently purchased from Northwick by the National Gallery in 1859 and
attributed to Botticelli in 1881. Julia Cartwright, in 1903, admired the young man for 'his bright
and pleasant countenance and keen intellectual air'. The painting used to be disfigured by black
spots on the flesh. It is likely that these were small bubbles which formed and burst during the
painting and filled with dirt over the centuries. During treatment it was found that the picture is,
unlike some others such as the early *Adoration of the Magi* (Plate 17), very simple in technique. The
flesh, for example, is of one paint layer only. The picture probably dates from the early 1480s.

(*above left*)
26 *Portrait of a Man with a Medal*
FLORENCE, Galleria degli Uffizi. Tempera on panel 57·5 × 44 cm.

The man holds a posthumous medal of Cosimo de' Medici, which is actually a cast set into the panel and gilded. Suggestions for the identification of the sitter, ranging from Pico della Mirandola to Botticelli's brother, are as varied as proposals for dating, from before 1470 to 1492. The man is very similarly dressed to that in the *Portrait of a Young Man* (Plate 25), but in almost every other respect the two pictures are quite unalike. The *Man with a Medal* has an air of vitality derived both from the pose of the figure, with the head turned slightly away from full face, and from the out-door setting, which makes the London *Young Man* appear rather stiff and two-dimensional by contrast.

(*above right*)
27 *Portrait of a Young Man Holding a Medallion*
LONDON, collection of Lady Merton, on loan to the National Gallery. Tempera on panel 58·4 × 39·4 cm.

Before entering the collection of Sir Thomas Merton, the picture belonged to Lord Newborough of Glynlivon Park, Caernarvon. It had been in the hands of his family since the time of the first Lord Newborough (1736–1807), who had lived for a time in Tuscany. The young man was identified by Scharf in a privately printed catalogue of the Merton collection (1950) as Giovanni di Pierfrancesco de' Medici (1467–1498), brother of Lorenzo di Pierfrancesco, but there is no real evidence to support this identification. The circular medallion fragment of an earlier picture, which is physically set into Botticelli's panel, has been attributed to the Ovile Master, dateable around 1350, in a note in the catalogue to an exhibition, *Italian Art in Britain*, at the Royal Academy, London, in 1960. The picture has not yet undergone technical tests, but when it does it may be possible to ascertain whether the inset fragment was put in the picture by Botticelli or whether the young man originally held a cast of a medal like the one in the Uffizi portrait (Plate 26).

(*above left*)
28 *Portrait of Giuliano de' Medici*
WASHINGTON, National Gallery of Art (Samuel H. Kress collection). Tempera on panel 75·6 × 52·6 cm. Cleaned 1950.

Formerly in the collection of Conte Vittorio Cini, Venice, this portrait passed through Wildenstein, New York, to Samuel Kress in 1949. Versions of the picture exist in the Staatliche Gemäldegalerie, Berlin (Dahlem), and in the Accademia Carrara, Bergamo and another, with the figure facing the left, is in the Crespi collection, Milan. Only the Washington picture has the dove on a dead branch in the foreground and the shuttered window, both symbols of death. Giuliano, the younger brother of Lorenzo 'il Magnifico', was murdered in Florence in 1478 at the age of twenty-five in the Pazzi conspiracy, possibly organized with the connivance of the della Rovere pope, Sixtus IV. He is shown in this picture in profile with downcast eyes as in *The Adoration of the Magi* (Plate 21), and it is possible that all four versions of the portrait are posthumous studies based on sources such as drawings for *The Adoration*. The Washington picture appears to be the most accomplished of the versions.

(*above right*)
29 *Portrait of Lorenzo Lorenzano*
PHILADELPHIA, Philadelphia Museum of Art (John G. Johnson collection). Tempera on panel 50·8 × 36·5 cm. Over-cleaned and extensively retouched.

The picture was purchased in 1909 by Johnson from Baron Lazzaroni, Paris, on the recommendation of Berenson. It is inscribed at the top: L. LORENTIANO. Lorenzano was a highly regarded scholar associated with the Medici circle. He held the chair of dialectics and then of physics and medicine at the University of Pisa. He committed suicide by throwing himself down a well in 1502. His date of birth is unknown. The picture is usually dated between 1485 and 1490.

The Sistine Chapel was built in Rome between 1475 and 1481, during the pontificate of Sixtus IV della Rovere, under the direction of the clerk of the works Giovanni dei Dolci, with Baccio Pontelli as architect. It is approximately forty metres long, thirteen metres wide and twenty-six metres high. Dolci was also responsible for overseeing the decoration, and it was he who in 1481 made arrangements with Botticelli, Ghirlandaio, Cosimo Roselli and Perugino to decorate the four walls with a frieze of scenes from the life of Moses and from the life of Christ and, between the windows, figures of martyred popes. There were originally sixteen principal scenes (see diagram). Four were finished by 17 January 1482 and a further ten by October 1482. The last two were executed by Signorelli who was probably brought in towards the end of 1482, after the other artists had left for Florence where on 5 October they were commissioned to paint the Sala dei Gigli of the Palazzo Vecchio. The ceiling of the Sistine Chapel was originally to have been a starry sky executed by the Umbrian painter Piermatteo d'Amelia, but there is no concrete evidence that it was ever executed. *The Life of Moses* scenes occupy the left side of the chapel. They began on the altar wall, now covered by Michelangelo's *Last Judgement*, with a *Finding of Moses* by Perugino, and ended on the opposite wall with a *Dispute over the Body of Moses* by Signorelli, later repainted by Matteo da Lecce. *The Life of Christ* scenes, arranged in typological sequence opposite *The Life of Moses*, began on the right of the altar wall with a *Nativity* by Perugino and ended with a *Resurrection* by Ghirlandaio, also repainted by Matteo da Lecce. The altarpiece was an *Assumption* by Perugino. Michelangelo's decorative scheme was commissioned during the pontificate (1503–13) of the second della Rovere pope, Julius II, and all that remains today of the original decoration from the time of Sixtus IV are the twelve scenes from *The Life of Moses* and *The Life of Christ* and the series of *Popes* on the lateral walls.

Diagram of the Original Scheme of the Sistine Chapel (not to scale)

Perugino The Finding of Moses (lost)	**Perugino** The Nativity (lost)

Perugino and Pinturicchio The Journey of Moses into Egypt	**ALTAR** **Perugino** The Assumption (lost)	**Perugino** The Baptism of Christ
Botticelli Moses in the Desert: his Vocation (Plate 31)		**Botticelli** The Temptation and the Purification of the Leper (Plate 33)
Cosimo Roselli The Passage of the Red Sea		**Ghirlandaio** The Vocation of Peter and Andrew
Cosimo Roselli (workshop) Moses and the Tables of the Law		**Cosimo Roselli and Piero di Cosimo** The Sermon on the Mount
Botticelli The Punishment of the Rebels (Plate V)		**Perugino** The Presentation of the Keys to Peter
Signorelli The Death of Moses		**Cosimo Roselli** The Last Supper

Signorelli The Dispute over the Body of Moses (lost)	**Ghirlandaio** The Resurrection (lost)

31 *Moses in the Desert: his Vocation*
VATICAN CITY, Sistine Chapel. Fresco 348·5 × 558 cm.

The Life of Moses series of frescoes reads from the altar from right to left. Botticelli's first contribution to the left wall is *Moses in the Desert*, the second fresco between *The Journey of Moses into Egypt* by Perugino and Pinturicchio and *The Passage of the Red Sea* by Cosimo Roselli (see diagram, p. 54). Botticelli depicted Moses seven times, first on the right, killing an Egyptian (Exodus II, 11 ff.) and then fleeing from Pharoah to the land of Midian where, by a well (centre) he drove away shepherds who had prevented the daughters of Jethro from watering their flock (Exodus II, 15 ff.). Jethro subsequently took Moses into his family, and it was while Moses was guarding Jethro's flock that God called to him from a burning bush (Exodus III, 1 ff.) and commanded him 'put off your shoes from your feet, for the place on which you are standing is holy ground'. The last episode represented by Botticelli is on the left, the return of Moses with his family to Egypt (Exodus IV, 19 ff.).

32 *Moses in the Desert: his Vocation* (detail of Plate 31)

33 *The Temptation and the Purification of the Leper*
VATICAN CITY, Sistine Chapel. Fresco 345·5 × 555 cm.

Although in theological terms the Moses story precedes and foreshadows the life of Christ, in the
Sistine Chapel, *The Life of Christ* on the right wall was painted first. Botticelli's *Temptation* is the
second fresco from the altar on the lateral wall directly opposite his *Moses in the Desert* (Plate 31)
(see diagram, p. 54). The temptations are depicted in the background. First, the devil, on the left,
subtly disguised in a monk's habit, attempts to persuade Christ to turn stones into bread
(Matthew IV, 1–4). He then (Matthew IV, 5–7) tries to cajole Christ into leaping from the
pinnacle of the Temple of Jerusalem, represented in the fresco as the Hospital of Santo Spirito,
built by Sixtus IV. Finally (top right), the devil is driven away after offering in vain all the king-
doms of the earth (Matthew IV, 8–11). The main scene in the foreground shows the leper cured by
Christ making an offering of thanksgiving (Matthew VIII, 1–4). Agostino Taja in his description of
the Vatican of 1750 noted especially how the figures in this fresco are all in 'belle attitudini'. Many
attempts have been made to identify figures in the composition with contemporaries and relations
of Pope Sixtus IV.

34 *The Temptation and the Purification of the Leper* (detail of Plate 33)

35   *The Punishment of the Rebels* (detail of Plate V)

(*opposite*)
V   *The Punishment of the Rebels*
VATICAN CITY, Sistine Chapel. Fresco 348·5 × 570 cm.

The Punishment of the Rebels is the fifth fresco on the left wall of the Sistine Chapel (see diagram, p. 54) and the most dramatic of the three by Botticelli. Korah and his sympathizers, who refuse to accept the authority of Aaron, are summoned by Moses to appear carrying censers before Aaron. On the right of the picture the followers of Moses and Aaron retreat as 'the earth opened up its mouth' and swallowed 'all the men that belonged to Korah and all their goods'. According to the Biblical source (Numbers XVI, 1–40) the confrontation took place at the entrance of a tent, but Botticelli placed it before the Arch of Constantine on which are emblazoned the words 'Nobody takes honour on himself unless like Aaron called by God' ('NEMO SIBI ASSUMM / AT HONOREM NISI VOCATUS A DEO / TANQUAM ARON').

(*page 62*)
VI   *St. Augustine in his Cell*
FLORENCE, Galleria degli Uffizi. Tempera on panel 41 × 27 cm.

In this picture a bright curtain is drawn back to give us a glimpse of a small ageing neighbourly figure only distantly related to the ecstatic *St. Augustine* of Ognissanti (Plate 37). It may be that the curtained-off sculptural setting was inspired by triumphal-arch style wall-tombs created earlier in the century by the Rosellino brothers, such as the Cardinal of Portugal's monument in San Miniato al Monte. The picture is believed to be the one mentioned by Vasari as by Filippo Lippi in the house of Bernardo Vecchietti. In the eighteenth century Ignazio Hugford of Florence sold it to Piero Pieralli, from whom it passed to the Uffizi in 1779.

(*above left*)
36 *St. Sixtus II* (detail)
VATICAN CITY, Sistine Chapel. Fresco 210 × 80 cm. (total measurement). Damaged and retouched.

Botticelli and his assistants had a hand in eleven of the twenty-eight existing *Popes* placed in painted niches at window level above the main frieze of scenes from *The Life of Moses* and *The Life of Christ*. Many of the *Popes* are badly damaged, and the *St. Sixtus* is repainted from the waist down and in details such as the hand, held to the breast in much the same attitude as that of the *St. Augustine* (Plate 37) of Ognissanti.

(*above right*)
37 *St. Augustine*
FLORENCE, refectory of the Monastery of Ognissanti. Fresco 152 × 112 cm.

Painted in 1480 for a member of the Vespucci family, perhaps Giorgio Antonio Vespucci, canon of the Cathedral of Florence, this fresco originally decorated the screen of the monks' choir in the Church of Ognissanti. When the screen and other mediaeval embellishments were removed under the direction of the Grand Duke Cosimo I de' Medici of Tuscany between 1564 and 1566 the *St. Augustine* and its pendant *St. Jerome* by Ghirlandaio were moved to the walls of the nave. The *St. Augustine* was set between the third and fourth altars on the right wall. After the 1564 detachment the inscription on the frieze was added: 'Augustine has devoted himself so completely to sacred studies that he is not aware that his location has been changed.' Since then he has moved again. Ognissanti was one of the many churches inundated by the disastrous flood of 1966 and although the *St. Augustine* and *St. Jerome* were not very seriously damaged, they were removed from the church, restored and repositioned on the right and left walls of the refectory, on either side of Ghirlandaio's famous *Last Supper*. The losses to the lower part of the draperies of *St. Augustine* are not flood damage; they are clearly visible in earlier photographs. Several scholars have proposed that both Botticelli's and Ghirlandaio's compositions may have been influenced by a small *St. Jerome in his Study* by van Eyck known to have been in the Medici collection in the fifteenth century but now lost.

38 '*La Derelicta*'
ROME, Galleria Pallavicini-Rospigliosi. Tempera on
panel 47·3 × 42·8 cm.

Although Federico Zeri's catalogue of the Galleria
Pallavicini of 1959 attributes the picture to Filippino
Lippi, most writers consider this mysterious little panel to
be by Botticelli. It was acquired by the Principe
Giuseppe Rospigliosi in 1816 as a work of Masaccio and
since that date numerous proposals for the identification
of the subject have been made, none of which can be
verified until some clue from the early history of the
picture is found.

(opposite top)
39 *Young Man before the Liberal Arts*
PARIS, Musée du Louvre. Fresco (detached) 227 × 269 cm. Extensively damaged.

In 1873 three frescoes were discovered under whitewash in the Villa Lemmi, a house in Chiasso
Macerelli, a road on the outskirts of Florence leading from near Ponte a Rifredi to San Pietro a
Careggi. One fresco, a ruin, remains in the villa, but the other two were moved to the Louvre in
1882 suffering damage in the process. The frescoes used to be associated with the marriage of
Giovanna degli Albizi and Lorenzo Tornabuoni in 1486 but several scholars, and principally
Gombrich, in 1945, have cast doubt on this connection, pointing out that the young woman in the
second fresco (Plate 40) does not resemble authentic representations of Giovanna, and that there is
no certainty that the Villa Lemmi ever belonged to the Tornabuoni family. Gombrich has also
drawn attention to a possible similarity between the rôle of Venus, here leading the young man
towards the liberal arts, and that of Venus of the *Primavera* (Plate 65) who acts as guide to
Humanitas for the young Lorenzo di Pierfrancesco de' Medici. Since the dating of 1486 can be discounted if the frescoes were not made for the Albizi-Tornabuoni marriage, a dating on the basis of
style can bring the picture earlier, nearer the time of the Sistine Chapel frescoes (Plates V and
30–36).

(opposite bottom)
40 *Young Woman Receives Gifts*
PARIS, Musée du Louvre. Fresco (detached) 212 × 284 cm. Extensively damaged.

Like the *Young Man before the Liberal Arts* (Plate 39) this fresco, which has the same provenance, has
suffered widespread damage and most of the *a secco* finishing is lost. The four figures to the left are
usually identified as Venus, presenting a gift to the young woman, and the three Graces, but as
with the first of the Villa Lemmi frescoes, the identification of the scene is far from clear.

65

43 *The Risen Christ Appears to Mary Magdalen ('Noli me Tangere')*
PHILADELPHIA, Philadelphia Museum of Art (John G. Johnson collection). Tempera on panel
18·5 × 42·3 cm.

Four predella panels depicting the life of Mary Magdalen survive in Philadelphia, *The Magdalen Listens to Christ Preaching*, *The Magdalen Washes Christ's Feet*, this *'Noli me Tangere'* and *The Magdalen's Communion and Ascension*. Horne found the panels with the dealer Luigi Grassi in Florence, and he recommended them to Johnson, believing them to be the predella of the *Madonna and Child Enthroned with Six Saints* (Plate 8) in the Uffizi. Roger Fry urged the Metropolitan Museum, New York, to buy them but they went to Johnson in 1908 for 160,000 lire. The lively handling suggests a date later than the *Madonna and Child Enthroned with Six Saints*, but it is not possible with present knowledge to associate the predella with any known altarpiece.

(opposite top)
41 *The Story of Virginia*
BERGAMO, Accademia Carrara. Tempera on panel 86 × 165 cm.

The Story of Virginia was purchased by Morelli at the Monte di Pietà, Rome, and lent by him as by Botticelli to an exhibition of Christian art in the Diocletian Baths in 1870. He bequeathed the picture to the Accademia Carrara in 1891. The *Virginia* and *Lucretia* (Plate 42) pictures are usually believed to be two elements in the decorative series commissioned by a member of the Vespucci family for their house in Via de' Servi. The paintings were probably designed by Botticelli and executed by his studio. Vasari reported, 'In Via de' Servi in the house of Giovanni Vespucci, now that of Piero Salviati, [Botticelli] painted round a room many pictures containing numerous lively figures framed in walnut for benchbacks and woodwork.' Guidantonio, not Giovanni, Vespucci purchased the Via de' Servi house in March 1499, and so the two pictures cannot have been painted before that date. *The Story of Virginia* is a legend of early Rome told by Livy in Book III of his *History*. Virginius kills his unfortunate daughter Virginia, to the right of the picture, rather than let her fall into the hands of Appius Claudius, in the centre, as his mistress or slave. The affair is said to have led to a revolution in 449 B.C. Livy's *History* was particularly admired by Dante.

(opposite bottom)
42 *The Story of Lucretia*
BOSTON, Isabella Stewart Gardner Museum. Tempera on panel 83·5 × 180 cm.

Acquired by Mrs. Gardner from the Earl of Ashburnham through Bernard Berenson in 1894, this panel is thought to have once decorated a room in the Vespucci home in Via de' Servi, together with *The Story of Virginia* (Plate 41). Lucretia, according to Livy's *History*, was raped by Sextus, son of Tarquinius Superbus. Rather than face the ensuing shame she kills herself (right).

44 *The Communion of St. Jerome*

NEW YORK, Metropolitan Museum of Art (bequest of Benjamin Altman). Tempera on panel 34·3 × 25·4 cm.

Another of Botticelli's smallest and most beautifully painted pictures, *The Communion of St. Jerome* is believed to have been painted for Francesco di Filippo del Pugliese, a wood-stapler and a follower of Savonarola. It was in the collection of the Marchese Gino Capponi, Florence, by 1841 and was inherited by the Marchese Farinola who sold it to Duveen, New York, in 1912. It was bequeathed by Altman to the Metropolitan in the following year. Botticelli's depiction of the last rites of the saint follows Buonacorsi's *Life of St. Jerome* published in Florence in 1490.

(*above*)
45 *Scenes from the Early Life of St. Zenobius*
LONDON, National Gallery. Tempera on panel 66·5 × 149·5 cm.

St. Zenobius, Bishop of Florence, is little known outside that city but scenes from his life have been depicted by a large number of artists including Ghirlandaio, Gozzoli, Veneziano and Ghiberti. The original home of Botticelli's four pictures on this theme is unknown but they must have formed a part of some decorative wall panelling scheme. The majority of critics suggest a late date for the group. The first set of scenes shows from the left, Zenobius renouncing the bride chosen for him, Zenobius being baptized by Theodosius, Bishop of Florence, the baptism of his mother, his consecration as Bishop of Florence by Pope St. Damasus. The stories in each case follow Tolosani's version of the legend, written in 1487. All four panels were in the Rondinelli collection, Florence, in the nineteenth century. This picture and the *Three Miracles of St. Zenobius* (Plate 46) were bought in 1891 for Dr. Ludwig Mond by J. P. Richter. They were part of the Mond bequest to the National Gallery in 1924.

(*overleaf top*)
46 *Three Miracles of St. Zenobius*
LONDON, National Gallery. Tempera on panel 65 × 139·5 cm.

On the left Zenobius exorcizes two young men, in the centre he restores to life a child who had died while left in his care, and on the right he brings sight to a blind beggar. The drawing of the figures is particularly vivid and fluent and parallels for several of them can be found in the illustrations to *La Divina Commedia* (Plates 70–73), though not in the examples illustrated in this book. The provenance for this picture is the same as that for the *Scenes from the Early Life of St. Zenobius* (Plate 45).

(*overleaf middle*)
47 *Four Miracles of St. Zenobius*
NEW YORK, Metropolitan Museum of Art (Kennedy fund). Tempera on panel 67·3 × 150·5 cm.
Restoration has revealed the coffin containing two corpses, formerly overpainted.

Like the London panels, this picture of the *St. Zenobius* series was in the Rondinelli collection, Florence, in the last century. It passed through the trade to Sir William Abdy, London, by 1885 and was sold by him at Christie's on 5 May 1911 to Langton Douglas. It was purchased by the Metropolitan Museum of Art in the same year. Zenobius on the left resuscitates one who had died, in the centre raises a young man, in the background cures a sick person and to the right empowers Deacon Eugenius to revive a woman.

(*overleaf bottom*)
48 *The Last Acts of St. Zenobius*
DRESDEN, Staatliche Gemäldegalerie. Tempera on panel 66 × 182 cm.

A child run over by a cart on the left is carried to Zenobius who revives him and restores him to his family. Finally, from his bed, the saint announces his approaching death. The panel went from the Rondinelli to the Metzger collection. It entered the Gemäldegalerie from the von Quandt collection in 1868.

49 *The First Episode of the Story of Nastagio degli Onesti*
MADRID, Museo del Prado. Tempera on panel 83 × 138 cm.

This panel is one of four scenes from the eighth tale of the fifth day of Boccaccio's *Decameron*, the first three of which are in the Prado, the fourth in an American private collection. It seems likely that the scenes were designed by Botticelli but executed by his studio. Vasari mentioned the four panels as being in the house of the Pucci family, Florence (see map, pp. 18–19), and Horne suggested that they were painted at the time of the wedding of Giannozzo Pucci and Lucrezia Bini in 1483. They remained with the Pucci until 1868 when they were sold to Barker, London and from there passed to Leyland; Aynard (1892); Spiridon, Paris; Cambo, Barcelona and the Prado. The fourth panel, after leaving Aynard went to Donaldson and then the Watney collection, Charlbury. Sir Charles Eastlake, who saw all four pictures at the Casa Pucci, calls the story 'repulsive' in his first notebook of 1861. Nastagio, in despair at being rejected by the daughter of Paolo Traversaro, wanders brooding on his ill-fortune through a pinewood at Chiassi, near Ravenna. Suddenly he encounters an apparition of a naked young woman being chased by dogs and a knight who, catching her, cuts out her heart and feeds it to the dogs. On hearing the story the young Traversaro girl, through fear of suffering a similar fate, bows to the wishes of Nastagio, and, recounted Boccaccio, ladies of Ravenna 'all became, and have ever since been, much more compliant with men's desires than they were wont to be'.

50 *The Raczinsky Tondo*
BERLIN (Dahlem), Staatliche Gemäldegalerie. Tempera on panel 135 cm. diameter. Damaged;
extensive retouching.

The picture was brought to Paris as Napoleonic booty and purchased there in 1824 by Count
Raczinsky of Berlin, passing from him to the Staatliche Gemäldegalerie. It is usually identified with
the tondo described by Vasari in the Church of San Francesco outside Porta San Miniato, now
known as San Salvatore al Monte (see map, pp. 18–19). Francesco Bocchi in *Le Bellezze di Firenze* (1591)
also recorded in the same church, 'In a chapel on the right hand side one sees a very beautiful
tondo by Sandro Botticelli', which, he added, was particularly admired by craftsmen: 'E stimata
molto questa pittura da gli Artefici'. The lily, which plays an important rôle in the composition of
this tondo, is symbolic of virginity and purity and as such is often associated with the Madonna in
Annunciations (Plates 56, 57 and VII) and other devotional pictures, such as *The Bardi Altarpiece*
(Plate 9). If the usual dating of 1475–80 is accepted the picture cannot originally have been made
for a site in the Church of San Salvatore which stands today, as the Franciscans only began work
on the church in 1487. The circular Madonna and Child theme was more often found in a domestic
setting or private chapel than in a church, but this picture must have looked well in its adoptive
home, San Salvatore being a Florentine building of unusual warmth, fondly called by Michelangelo 'the pretty country lass'.

51 *Madonna of the Magnificat*
FLORENCE, Galleria degli Uffizi. Tempera on panel 118 cm. diameter. Damage and retouching on the faces of the Madonna and the Christ Child.

John Addington Symonds in 1877 called this Botticelli's 'best known picture'. He believed it combined 'all Botticelli's best qualities. For rare distinction of beauty in the faces it is unique, while the mystic calm and resignation, so misplaced in his Aphrodites, find a meaning here'. The picture was acquired by the Uffizi as an anonymous work in 1784 from Ottavio Margherini and attributed to Botticelli in the nineteenth century, probably first by Cavalcaselle in 1864. The Madonna is shown writing the Magnificat (Luke I, 46–55), while being crowned by angels. The picture is usually dated in the 1480s, and the highly polished technique renders it comparable with *The Bardi Altarpiece* (Plate 9) of 1484–85. It has frequently suffered from being reproduced at an angle without a proper regard for the lines of the distant landscape. A number of variant copies exist.

52 *Madonna of the Pomegranate*
FLORENCE, Galleria degli Uffizi. Tempera on panel 143·5 cm. diameter.

Although the design of this tondo of the mid-1480s is a restatement of the composition of *The
Raczinsky Tondo* (Plate 50), certain telling details such as the hands of the Madonna, which in the
earlier picture were thin and angular, have changed fundamentally with the maturing of the artist's
style. The angels have graduated from a rather indolent human crowd to a more heavenly winged
group who actively contribute to the tondo composition by pressing in on the Madonna and Child
instead of leaning out against the circumference of the panel as they did in *The Raczinsky Tondo*.
The pomegranate, also used by Botticelli in his early *Madonna and Child in an Archway* (Plate 2) and
in the *Madonna of the Magnificat* (Plate 51), is an ancient Semitic symbol of fertility and regeneration
sometimes translated into a Christian image of immortality. The picture was listed in 1675 among
the possessions of Cardinal Leopoldo de' Medici, from whom it went to the Medici grand dukes and
then to the Uffizi in 1780. It may have been the tondo painted for the audience chamber of the
Magistrato de' Massai della Camera in the Palazzo della Signoria in 1487.

53 *Madonna and Child with Three Angels*
MILAN, Pinacoteca Ambrosiana. Tempera on panel 65 cm. diameter.

It is possible that this, much the smallest of Botticelli's tondo pictures, was the one seen by Vasari in the Monastery of Santa Maria degli Angeli in Via degli Alfani (see map, pp. 18–19) which was suppressed in 1808. Even if it were not this picture it would admirably fit Vasari's description of a painting 'made with beautiful care'. It has always been accepted as a late work of the 1490s.

(above left)
54 *The Finding of the Dead Holofernes*
FLORENCE, Galleria degli Uffizi. Tempera on panel 31 × 25 cm.

The picture probably formed a diptych with *The Return of Judith* (Plate 55). They were given by
Rodolfo Sirigatti to Bianca Cappello, second wife of the Grand Duke Francesco I de' Medici around
1580. Her son Antonio inherited them and at his death in 1632 the panels went to the Uffizi.
Judith, a young widow from Bethulia, a town besieged by the Babylonians, deceived Holofernes the
Babylonian general into believing her to be an ally. Every night she crossed the siege lines to visit
his tent until one night his drunken sleep gave her the opportunity to murder him and thus secure
the collapse of the siege. Judging from the figure types the pictures must date from the period of
the two early *Adoration* pictures in the National Gallery, London (Plates 17 and III): the man to the
back on the right in this picture who looks upward and raises his arm to shield the light from his
eyes has a parallel in the figure on the extreme left of the rectangular London *Adoration* (Plate 17).
The body of Holofernes is Botticelli's earliest known attempt at portraying a male nude. A more
accomplished rendering of the male torso can be seen in the *Venus and Mars* (Plate 61) and the
Munich *Pietà* (Plate 58).

(above right)
55 *The Return of Judith*
FLORENCE, Galleria degli Uffizi. Tempera on panel 31 × 24 cm.

The delicate grey and chalky blue colour scheme of Judith's dress helps to make this the prettiest
of Botticelli's early pictures, despite the gruesome subject matter. The foot of Judith was originally
painted further to the right. It was probably altered by Botticelli so that the line of her leg should
not echo exactly that of the forward stepping leg of the maid. Judith carries an olive branch very
similar to those held by figures in *The Mystic Nativity* (Plate IV). The branch was presumably
intended to signify that Judith, on her return to Bethulia with the head of Holofernes, was bringing
peace to the city. Another small panel of *Judith with the Head of Holofernes* by Botticelli is in the
Rijksmuseum, Amsterdam. It has been cut down and is very damaged.

56 *The Annunciation*
NEW YORK, Metropolitan Museum of Art (Robert Lehman collection). Tempera on panel 24 × 36 cm.

This small *Annunciation* was given with the Lehman collection to the Metropolitan Museum in 1969. Previously it had belonged to Huldschinsky of Berlin and the Barberini collection, Rome. Its earlier history is unknown. Despite the grandeur of the architecture the scene is realized as an intimate domestic interior. The curtain serves a similar function to the one in the *St. Augustine in his Cell* (Plate VI), a picture of about the same size. Suggestions for dating the picture differ very greatly. All that can be said with a degree of certainty is that it must be before the Glasgow *Annunciation* (Plate VII), which dates from around 1500. By comparison with the Glasgow picture the architecture is rather cramped and the figures lacking in grace and balance. In the Lehman *Annunciation* the wings of the angel are rather awkwardly made to follow the lines of the rays representing the entrance of the Holy Spirit, with the result that the angel appears to be toppling forward and looking at the floor rather than towards the Virgin. No such problems exist in the Glasgow picture.

(*overleaf*)
57 *The Annunciation*
FLORENCE, Galleria degli Uffizi. Tempera on panel 150 × 156 cm.

This picture was made for the chapel of Benedetto Guardi, the second from the right in the Church of Santa Maria Maddelena de' Pazzi in Florence. According to the *libro de' benefattori* of the church, quoted by Horne, the chapel was built between March 1489 and June 1490, and the altarpiece which was made during this period cost thirty ducats. The empty room in which the scene takes place and the landscape background differ very greatly from the architectural settings of the Lehman and Glasgow pictures and appear to reflect a knowledge of Flemish models. The rather stiff and dry handling of the picture led Horne to the conclusion that it was a studio work. Although it may have been in part painted by studio hands the conception must have been Botticelli's and a similar style can be seen in the two *Pietà* pictures (Plates 58 and 59) and the *Pentecost* (Plate 60). This rather bland manner in which the artist occasionally worked is hard to characterize, but if the Uffizi *Annunciation* is compared with a picture on a similar scale, such as *The Bardi Altarpiece* (Plate 9), it can be seen that *The Annunciation* suffers from a dearth of ornamentation both in costumes and the setting. *The Annunciation* was found in 1870 in a chapel near Fiesole belonging to the nuns of Santa Maria Maddelena de' Pazzi and was taken to the Uffizi in 1872.

(*opposite*)

VII *The Annunciation*

GLASGOW, City Art Gallery and Museum. Tempera on panel 51 × 61 cm., including narrow strips added at top and bottom. Extensive retouching.

The provenance of this, the latest of Botticelli's Annunciations has recently been traced by Martin Kemp. From the evidence of an old inscription on the back of the panel he has shown that the picture was originally in the Church of San Barnaba, Florence, which also housed *The San Barnaba Altarpiece* (Plate 10). The picture was purchased in the early 1830s by the Revd. John Sandford from the Casa Rivani in Florence and sold in 1839 to a 'Davis' for £4 12s. It subsequently entered the collection of Archibald McLellan of Glasgow and then in 1856, two years after his death, became the property of the Glasgow Corporation. The picture was on public view in the McLellan Galleries, Glasgow from 1855 to 1902, when it was moved to its present home. Like *The Agony in the Garden* (Plate 24) it has suffered a lack of serious recognition because of its somewhat out of the way location. When seen in the original the high quality of the picture is apparent despite its unhappy condition. It is equal in intensity of expression to works such as the Dante drawings and *The Mystic Nativity* (Plate IV). As in the Dante illustrations the setting plays a part in the narrative. As Martin Kemp has observed, Botticelli actually moved the lines of the architecture out of perpendicular during the course of painting in order to emphasize the narrative flow of the subject. The central column, for example, inclines towards the entrance of the angel on the left. Botticelli's versions of the Annunciation illustrated here do not form a coherent group in the way that, for instance, the Adoration pictures do, mainly because the Uffizi *Annunciation* (Plate 57) has such an entirely different kind of setting from the other two and is also a great deal larger in scale.

58 *Pietà*

MUNICH, Alte Pinakothek. Tempera on panel 139·5 × 207·3 cm.

The picture was bought by Crown Prince Ludwig of Bavaria, later Ludwig I, in 1814 from the Church of San Paolino very near Botticelli's home in Florence (see map, pp. 18–19). It passed into the possession of the Bavarian state in 1850, and although it has hung as a Botticelli in the Alte Pinakothek since 1836 a number of scholars have questioned the extent of Botticelli's participation. To the eye accustomed to the decorative appeal of such popular pictures as the *Madonna of the Magnificat* (Plate 51), the rather bland areas of colour are somewhat disconcerting but the artist employed a rather similar style in several other pictures of his later period, notably in the Birmingham *Pentecost* (Plate 60) and the Uffizi *Annunciation* (Plate 57) commissioned in 1489. In the case of the *Pietà* he could well have considered a plainer style to be in sympathy with the subject. The pathos of the scene is heightened by the contrast between the pale, youthful body and beardless face of Christ and the rugged figures of the three older saints who look on. The Christ is very close to the Mars of *Venus and Mars* (Plate 61) in the National Gallery, London. The picture probably dates from the early 1490s, less than a decade before Michelangelo's St. Peter's *Pietà*.

(*opposite*)
VIII *Venus and Mars* (see Plate 61)

60 *Pentecost*

BIRMINGHAM, City Art Gallery. Tempera on panel 221 × 229 cm. Numerous losses and old retouchings; restored 1973.

The picture was purchased by Birmingham in 1959 from Julius Weitzer after an export licence had been refused to Bob Jones University, Greenville, South Carolina. Mandel and Salvini mistakenly catalogue it as at Greenville. Earlier the *Pentecost* had been in the Cook collection, Richmond and immediately before that, until 1874, with the Abbé Hyeres at the Jesuit College, Lyons. He had purchased it in 1872 from Michele and Luigi Gamberini who believed it to be *The Convertite Altarpiece* (cf, Plate 8). The subject is from Acts II, 1–4: 'they were all together in one place. And suddenly a sound came from heaven like the rush of a mighty wind, and it filled all the house where they were sitting. And there appeared to them tongues as of fire, distributed and resting on each one of them. And they were all filled with the Holy Spirit . . .' Cannon-Brookes has pointed out that the composition follows a type usually found in miniatures. The subject is rarely found on any larger scale but the great round window of Santo Spirito is decorated with a *Pentecost* designed by Perugino in about 1500. In Perugino's composition the Apostles are similarly grouped in a circle round the Virgin, but they are standing rather than seated. Botticelli's picture is probably slightly earlier than the window design, dating from the period between the Munich and the Panciatichi *Pietà*s (Plates 58 and 59) and *The Mystic Nativity* (Plate IV).

(*opposite*)
59 *The Panciatichi Pietà*

MILAN, Museo Poldi-Pezzoli. Tempera on panel 107 × 71 cm. Restored 1951; extensive overpainting removed.

Like the early *St. Sebastian* (Plate 7) this panel hung on one of the pillars in Santa Maria Maggiore. Vasari mentioned it in the second edition of his *Vite* (1568), 'at the side of the Chapel of the Panciatichi' ('allato capella di Panciatichi'). The picture was in the sacristy by 1755. The Museo Poldi-Pezzoli acquired it from the antiquarian Baslini in 1855. Only since restoration has it emerged as an undoubted autograph work of Botticelli related in style and probably in date to the Munich *Pietà* (Plate 58). A bad copy in the Bautier collection, Brussels, has sometimes mistakenly been associated with Botticelli's studio.

(opposite top)
61 *Venus and Mars* (see Plate VIII)
LONDON, National Gallery. Tempera on panel 69 × 173.5 cm.

Botticelli's only major mythological picture to be found outside Italy, *Venus and Mars* was purchased between 1864 and 1869 by Alexander Barker in Florence and bought by the National Gallery at the Barker sale in 1874. There is no record of its earlier provenance, but Gombrich has suggested that the wasps (*vespe*) near Mars's head may refer to the Vespucci family by whom Botticelli is known to have been employed (cf. Plates 41 and 42). There can be no definitive analysis of the subject, but it appears to be Love, personified by Venus, transcending War, Mars, asleep and disarmed by satyrs. The picture must date from the mid to late 1480s. The Venus is very close in type to the St. Catherine of *The San Barnaba Altarpiece* (Plate 10) of 1488–90. John Addington Symonds harboured an irrational dislike for the picture and for Mars in particular: 'The face and attitude of that unseductive Venus . . . opposite her snoring lover, seems to symbolise the indignities which women have to endure from insolent and sottish boys with only youth to recommend them.'

(opposite bottom)
62 *Venus and Mars* (actual-size detail of Plate 61)

(overleaf)
63 *Pallas and the Centaur*
FLORENCE, Galleria degli Uffizi. Tempera on canvas 207 × 148 cm. Probably transferred from panel.

This picture has had a chequered history. It was once at Castello in the collection of Lorenzo and Giovanni di Pierfrancesco de' Medici and then in that of Giovanni 'delle Bande Nere' de' Medici. It was still at Castello in 1638 but went to the Palazzo Pitti around 1830. It was 'rediscovered' in about 1893 in, according to Julia Cartwright, 'a dark corner of the Pitti Palace', and moved to the Uffizi. Its appearance is marred today by the presence of numerous faded retouchings covering most areas of the canvas. The dress of Pallas is decorated with the personal badge of Lorenzo 'il Magnifico'. Several political interpretations of the picture have been proposed but latterly scholars have preferred to see it as related to Marsilio Ficino's concept of the duality of the soul, half-animal and sensual and half-human and capable of reason. Pallas Athena or Minerva, Wisdom, guides or restrains the centaur, a creature of visibly dual nature.

(page 87)
64 *The 'Calumny' of Apelles*
FLORENCE, Galleria degli Uffizi. Tempera on panel 62 × 91 cm.

Lucian, the Greek writer of the second century A.D., described in detail the *Calumny* painted by his compatriot Apelles in the fourth century B.C. Apelles was the official painter to the Macedonian court and reputedly the only man allowed to portray Alexander the Great. Alberti paraphrased Lucian's description in his *De Pictura*, Book III, paragraph 53, thus: 'In the painting there was a man with enormous ears sticking out, attended on each side by two women, Ignorance and Suspicion; from one side Calumny was approaching in the form of an attractive woman, but whose face seemed too well versed in cunning, and she was holding in her left hand a lighted torch, while with her right she was dragging by the hair a youth with his arms outstretched towards heaven. Leading her was another man, pale, ugly and fierce to look upon, whom you would rightly compare to those exhausted by long service in the field. They identified him correctly as Envy. There are two other women attendant on Calumny and busy arranging their mistress's dress; they are Treachery and Deceit. Behind comes Repentance clad in mourning and rending her hair, and in her train chaste and modest Truth.' The sculptural setting in Botticelli's painting was probably intended to evoke the spirit of a classical age, but the figures and reliefs do not relate stylistically to known classical pieces, and they represent a miscellany of subjects both Christian and mythological. The figure of St. George in the niche on the central column appears to be derived from Andrea Castagno's *Pippo Spano* fresco in Sant' Apollonia, Florence. The figure of 'Modest Truth' on the left, like the Venus of *The Birth of Venus* (Plate 66), is related to the classical sculpture *Venus Pudica*. Proposals for dating this picture vary between 1485 and 1495. It was presented by Botticelli to Antonio Segni of Florence, according to Vasari, who saw it in his son Fabio Segni's house. It passed to the Pitti and then in 1773 to the Uffizi.

(*overleaf*)
65 *Primavera* (*Spring*)
FLORENCE, Galleria degli Uffizi. Tempera on panel 203 × 314 cm.

Lorenzo di Pierfrancesco de' Medici, who inherited a fortune at the death of his father Pierfrancesco in 1476, acquired the Villa di Castello in 1477 and may have had the *Primavera* executed for this, his country home, in the following year. Interpretations of the subject of the picture are legion. Vasari rather inaccurately calls it 'a Venus, whom the Graces are covering with flowers ['lo fioriscono'] denoting spring'. As in two of the Sistine frescoes the theme (it can hardly be called narrative) reads from right to left. The impetus is given by Zephyr who blows from the right. On the left, Mercury, associated with the month of May, turns as if to indicate the passage of spring towards summer. Zephyr's breath causes flowers to spring from the mouth of the earth nymph Chloris, who then assumes the richly-clad form of Flora as the next figure in the group. Venus, the personification of April, stands in the centre of the picture gesturing towards her attendant Graces. The picture is dulled and darkened by surface dirt. It generally appears more colourful in reproduction than 'in the flesh' as the powerful lighting needed to photograph such a dark image penetrates the dust and grime. The picture remained at Castello until 1815, when it was transferred to the Uffizi. It was in the Accademia for a spell until 1919.

66 *The Birth of Venus* (see Plate II)
FLORENCE, Galleria degli Uffizi. Tempera on canvas 172·5 × 278·5 cm. Probably transferred from panel; damage along a horizontal join across the centre of the canvas has been crudely retouched.

The Birth of Venus is Botticelli's best known and most popular work, painted, like the *Primavera* (Plate 65), for the Villa di Castello, though not as a pendant of the earlier picture. The provenance of both paintings is the same. The theme may be related to the Neo-Platonist education of the young Lorenzo di Pierfrancesco de' Medici for whom it was painted. Letters from the tutor Marsilio Ficino to Lorenzo show that Venus was imagined not as an erotic figure but as a symbol of *Humanitas*, an image of beauty intended to inspire men's most noble thoughts. The picture represents Venus's spiritual birth: when Saturn castrated Heaven and threw the testicles into the sea Venus was born from the foam. *The Birth of Venus* was painted after Botticelli's return from Rome, in the mid-1480s.

(*opposite*)
67 *The Birth of Venus* (detail of Plate 66)

68 *Three Angels*

FLORENCE, Galleria degli Uffizi, Gabinetto dei Disegni e Stampe. Pen and ink on brown tinted paper, heightened with white 10·2 × 23·5 cm.

Yashiro called this 'the finest example of the precision and purity of the Quattrocento drawing'.

69 *Abundance*

LONDON, British Museum, Department of Prints and Drawings. Pen and ink and wash over black chalk with white heightening on tinted paper 31·7 × 25·3 cm.

Vasari recorded that he had in his collection several drawings by Botticelli. When Horne saw the *Abundance* it was set in what he believed to be one of Vasari's mounts, but this has since disappeared. In its more recent history it was sold by Rogers at Christie's, London in 1856 as by Verrocchio, and subsequently owned by Morris, Moore, Sir J. C. Robinson and Malcolm, from whom it passed to the British Museum in 1895. The British Museum cataloguers believe it to date from shortly after the *Primavera* (Plate 65), while Horne and others place it after Botticelli's visit to Rome.

70 *La Divina Commedia, Inferno, Canto I*
VATICAN CITY, Biblioteca Apostolica Vaticana. Silverpoint, pen and ink on vellum 32 × 47 cm.

Botticelli designed a number of illustrations for Cristoforo Landino's 1481 edition of Dante's *La Divina Commedia*. Nineteen of these were crudely engraved by Baccio Baldini (cf. fig. 14), and we can only guess at the quality of the original drawings as they are apparently all lost. The magnificent series of drawings which survive in Rome and Berlin is believed to be that which the Anonimo Gaddiano recorded was made for Lorenzo di Pierfrancesco de' Medici. Horne, noting that Lorenzo fled from Florence in 1497, concluded that the drawings must have been complete by that date, but Yashiro, calling them 'the beautiful suicide of Botticelli's art', placed them among the very latest of the artist's works. The Vatican sheets (Cantos I and IX–XVI) of the *Inferno* were acquired from Queen Christina's estate in 1690. It is not known where they were earlier. *Inferno, Canto I* is the beginning of *La Divina Commedia*. Dante, after wandering lost in a forest, finds himself at the foot of a hill over which the sun is just rising. Attempting to climb the hill, he is driven back by a panther, a lion and a wolf. In fear he turns back to the forest, but his course is changed, and the whole story set in motion, by the appearance of Virgil, who volunteers to be his guide. Beatrice hovers in the sky above. The engraving of *Inferno, Canto I* in Landino's *Divina Commedia* is close in design to this drawing.

71 *La Divina Commedia, Inferno, Canto XII*
VATICAN CITY, Biblioteca Apostolica Vaticana. Silverpoint, pen and ink on vellum 32 × 47 cm.

Descending a rocky path Dante and Virgil encounter the Minotaur, whom Virgil orders aside so
that they can pass. They reach a ditch filled with blood in which flounder the souls of the damned.
Virgil persuades one of the herd of centaurs, who are shooting arrows at the souls, to accompany
him and Dante as a guide. As in the majority of the illustrations, the protagonists, Dante and
Virgil, appear more than once in the picture. The engraving of the same canto in the Landino
edition of *La Divina Commedia* incorporates a portion of this design in reverse.

72 *La Divina Commedia, Inferno, Canto XVI*
VATICAN CITY, Biblioteca Apostolica Vaticana. Silverpoint, pen and ink on vellum 32 × 47 cm.

Dante and Virgil come upon a band of sodomites doing penance in a sea of sand and shower of flames. Virgil tells Dante to unfasten the belt from his waist and lower it into the ditch where the monster Geryon, in the lower left corner, rises up and supports himself in front of them. Usurers, each with a pouch round his neck, sit at the edge of the precipice under a shower of flame. This scene, like the preceding two illustrated here (Plates 70 and 71), has a counterpart in Landino's *Divina Commedia*, but the composition in this case is quite different.